BOOK SYNOPSIS

This book provides foundational truths of the relevancy and importance of apostles today. It reveals biblical and spiritual facts regarding the character, nature, identity, calling, and mantle of an apostle. It equips the apostle with keys to effectively embrace, wear, cultivate, and operate in the mantle of their calling; while yielding revelation that apostolic people, ministries, organizations, and businesses can glean from as they work with apostles for the equipping, training, building up, and advancement of the kingdom of God. Throughout this book, Taquetta and her spiritual daughter, Nina Cook, will share their apostolic journey. They create a contrast between the wounded and healed apostle to help the reader receive keys and revelation for properly wearing their apostolic mantle.

The Apostolic Mantle:

Foundational Truths On How To Wear Your Calling

TaquettaBaker@Kingdomshifters.com

(Website) Kingdomshifters.com

Connect with Taquetta via Facebook or YouTube

Copyright 2017 – Kingdom Shifters Ministries

All rights reserved. This book is protected by the copyright laws of the United States of America. This book may not be reprinted for commercial gain or profit. The use of occasional page copying for personal or group study is permitted and encouraged. Permission will be granted upon request.

Taquetta's Bio

Taquetta Baker is the founder of Kingdom Shifters Ministries (KSM). She has authored fourteen books and two decree CD's. Taquetta has a Master's Degree in Community Counseling with an emphasis on Marriage, Children and Family Counseling, a Bachelor's Degree in Psychology and Associates Degree in Business Administration. In addition, Taquetta has a Therapon Belief Therapist Certification from Therapon Institute and has 22 years of professional and Christian Counseling experience.

Taquetta is also gifted at empowering and assisting people with launching ministries, businesses and books and provides mentoring, counseling and vision casting through Kingdom Shifters Kingdom Wellness Program. Taquetta serves on the Board of Directors for New Day Community Ministries, Inc. of Muncie, IN. In October 2008, Taquetta graduated from the Eagles Dance Institute under Dr. Pamela Hardy and received her license in the area of liturgical dance. Before launching into her own ministry, Taquetta served at her previous church for 12 years. She was a prophet, pioneer and leader of Shekinah Expressions Dance Ministry, teacher, member of the presbytery board, and overseer of the Altar Workers

Ministry. Taquetta receives mentoring and ministry covering from Bishop Jackie Green, Founder of JGM-Enternational PrayerLife Institute (Redlands, AZ), and was ordained as an Apostle on June 7, 2014.

Taquetta flows through the wells of warfare and worship and mantles an apostolic mandate of judging and establishing God's kingdom in people, ministries, communities, and regions. Taquetta travels in foreign missions and throughout the United States. She has mentored and established dance, altar workers, deliverance, and prophetic ministries. Taquetta ministers in the areas of fine arts, all manners of prayer, fivefold ministry, deliverance, healing, miracles, atmospheric worship, and empowers and train people in their destiny and life's vision.

Connect with Taquetta and KSM at kingdomshifters.com or via Facebook. For more information regarding Bishop Jackie Green at Jgmenternational.org.

Nina's Bio

Nina Cook has been saved since childhood and has been active in ministry much of her life. Nina carries an apostolic mantle with giftings in dance, singing, production, all manner of prayer, spiritual warfare, deliverance, healing, teaching, pastoring, scribing, and wellness. Nina graduated from Ball State University in 2014 with a Bachelor's Degree concentration in Exercise Science and a Minor in Dance. Nina has over 5 years of experience in the wellness and exercise field and 11 years and counting of dance experience.

Nina is an Elder at Kingdom Shifters Christian Empowerment Center in Muncie, Indiana. She is the main armor bearer for her pastor and is also training in her calling as an apostle. Nina is the founder of "Manifold Grace Production Company" and "Exercise to Life." It is her vision that her production company brings transformation to people and regions through the power and creativity of the arts. Nina is an extraordinary teacher and minister of movement, choreography, atmospheric worship, and using dance and movement in warfare and intercession. Nina provides fitness coaching and exercise and dance class through "Exercise to Life." She utilizes a vast variety of exercise and *fitness styles that people can do that are combined with scriptural focuses, short teachings, prayers, and declarations and decrees such that when people do the exercises their bodies are transformed. It is her vision to see people transformed through bringing healing and deliverance to the physical body in areas that hinder their health and wellness, and to also see complete lifestyle changes that shift people into wholeness.*

Nina is dedicated to living her life sold out to Christ. She is generally the first to volunteer and take risks for anything that grows the kingdom. She is always seeking to learn, develop, and cultivate herself in the integrity, character, fruit and will of God.

Connect with Nina and Manifold Grace Production Company and "Exercise to Life" at Manifoldgrace5@gmail.com, kingdomshifters.com or via Facebook, and Youtube.

Forward

THIS BOOK IS AN APOSTOLIC TREASURE CHEST! IT IS FULL OF RICHES OF WISDOM, PRACTICAL HELPS, STRATEGIES AND REAL LIFE TESTIMONIES FOR APOSTLES AND APOSTLES-IN-THE-MAKING. THIS BOOK GIVES VALID AND CAREFUL WISDOM ON HOW TO WALK IN YOUR APOSTLESHIP CALLING STEP BY STEP. AS ONE OF TAQUETTA'S SPIRITUAL APOSTOLIC MOTHERS, I CAN SAY THE BODY OF CHRIST IS IN GOOD HANDS WITH SUCH BALANCED TEACHING. THIS BOOK WILL HELP RAISE UP MANY GENERATIONS OF TRUE APOSTLES FOR THE KINGDOM OF GOD.

THIS BOOK CAN BE APPLIED TO THE PROPHETIC CALLING AS WELL. I WAS REFRESHED AND GIRDED UP IN MY OWN APOSTOLIC CALLING. I RECEIVED A PERSONAL INJECTION OF FRESH APOSTOLIC REVELATION THAT ENRICHED MY OWN APOSTOLIC MANTLE.

<u>THE APOSTOLIC MANTLE</u> WRITTEN BY APOSTLE TAQUETTA BAKER IS A MASTERPIECE FROM THE HEART OF THE MASTER, JESUS CHRIST. HE HAS IMPRINTED UPON THE HEART OF THIS YOUNG AUTHOR THE BLUEPRINTS FOR ANYONE CALLED TO MINISTRY, BUT IN THIS CASE, THE APOSTLESHIP OF JESUS CHRIST. THE APOSTLESHIP IS A PRECIOUS MINISTRY GIVEN BY THE LORD JESUS CHRIST TO THOSE HE HAS CHOSEN AND GIFTED.

THE AUTHOR SHARES THE IMPORTANCE OF SEEKING GOD FOR THE DEFINITION AND IDENTITY OF THEIR APOSTOLIC CALL AND NOT HATING THE LOCAL CHURCH FOR NOT EMBRACING THEIR CALLING AND BUT GETTING HEALED FROM ALL BITTERNESS AND WOUNDEDNESS.

FINALLY, I LOVED HOW THIS BOOK ADDRESSED, THE "YOUNGENS" WHICH IS PART OF EVERY TRUE *APOSTLE'S CALLING*. APOSTLE TAQUETTA SAYS: *"Now in 2017 we are calling these same youngens Millennials. Challengingly, now we have a host of Millennials who are angry at the church and* leaders, do not want to go to church, and are rebellious against doctrine and anything that would try to put them in a box. • Millennials who are dying in dead churches that refuse to SHIFT the baton to them. They are so loyal they cannot get themselves to leave despite knowing they are spiritually dead and that the church is stuck, idle, and DEAD! • Millennials who are anointed but rebellious; they are starting their own ministries, yet still bound in sin, worldliness, church hurt, etc.; they put a worldly twist on the things of God then rebelliously STRIKE against the saints who call out their unrighteousness. • Millennials who are ON FIRE FOR GOD! They know they are called and want what God has for them. Some of them have spiritual parents, mentors, and leaders who have gotten a clue and are helping them SHIFT into their identity and calling. They are stumbling and fumbling, but their hearts are pure for the Lord and the things of God."

THIS BOOK IS FOR THE APOSTLES OF THE FUTURE AS WELL AS FOR TODAY. I THANK GOD FOR WHAT MY EYES AND EARS AND HEART HAVE EXPERIENCED IN THIS RICH APOSTOLIC WORK. THANK YOU APOSTLE TAQUETTA FOR BIRTHING THIS BOOK FORTH AND FOR ALREADY MOTHERING THE APOSTOLIC AND PROPHETIC GENERATIONS!

BISHOP DR. JACKIE L. GREEN, FOUNDER/OVERSEER, JGM ENTERNATIOAL PRAYER LIFE INSTITUTE

REDLANDS, CALIFORNIA

Forward

When Jesus was born, He came in the form of man. As a baby, He cried when He was hungry, wet and in need of comfort. As a toddler, He learned to crawl, walk and talk. As a pre-teen, He learned Joseph's trade of carpentry. He was an obedient child. When He was twelve, He was found in the temple asking and answering questions among the teachers. At this time Jesus was totally persuaded and confident of His God nature. He knew that God was His Father.

No one is born with the knowledge of their God-given purpose and destiny. We have to discover the seeds planted in us by God. In our discovery, God begins to reveal times and seasons when our seeds began budding. As we desire to live our lives in the will of God, we begin earnestly seeking His face. This earnest seeking brings with it many different emotions, actions and reactions. There are days of excitement, nervousness, confidence, uncertainty, boldness and wavering. Our actions follow every instruction we hear from the voice of God. But the reaction of others toward us is jealousy, anger and disapproval. We seem double-minded.

The Apostolic Mantle: Foundational Truths on How to Wear Your Calling will assist in understanding this process for the apostle. This book is filled with confirmation and revelation. The "Exploration Questions and Nuggets" gives you an opportunity to ponder your personal journey. While the "Apostolic Prayers" empower you to speak and command your spirit to align with God and SHIFT!! There are moments of:

"I can see when that happened in my life"
"Yes, this is who I am"
"Ouch, I have to change in this area"

Apostle Taquetta Baker is very transparent on her journey to the apostolic. She gives you a clear picture of the struggles, triumphs and inner spiritual battles. She also assures you that God has ordained and designed your journey to fit your mantle. She uncovers the myths of biblical schooling, being confirmed by men and supporting the apostolic call. Apostle Taquetta identifies the different types of warfare that apostles encounter. But she also establishes the importance of living a refreshed life. This will keep the apostle always ready for the next level of warfare.

Apostle Nina Cook's insightful revelation and journey is key to understanding the covering, mentoring and training in the apostolic. She gives a glimpse inside the on-the-job training that never stops. She explains vividly on learning in many different areas at one time. Learning to multi-task and use wisdom on what is needed in each situation is taught as they arise. She gleans many life lessons, training and strength from her mentor, Apostle Taquetta Baker.

If your calling is apostolic, this book will confirm and affirm who you are and how God desires you to operate in the Kingdom of God. It will equip you in understanding your strengths and weaknesses. You will be empowered to stay connected to God the Father, God the Son and God the Holy Spirit. Activate your prayers and decrees to stir up your spirit in your specific warfare calling. SHIFT and walk in your Apostolic mantle.

Apostle Renee Gray
Restored to Purpose Ministry
Praise Party School of Dance

Table of Contents

INTRODUCTION INTO APOSTLESHIP 1
THE APOSTOLIC CALL 4
GOD ORCHESTRATES THE CALL 12
FOUNDATION & RELEVANCY Of APOSTLESHIP 19
CHARACTERISTICS OF AN APOSTLE 28
NATURE OF AN APOSTLE 31
THE IDENTITY OF AN APOSTLE 49
THE APOSTOLIC MANTLE 61
UNHEALTHY VERSUS HEALED APOSTLE 81
UNCONFIRMED VERSUS CONFIRMED AS AN APOSTLE...95
BLIND DESTINY VISION VERSUS CLEAR DESTINY VISION..102
JOY VERSUS TOLERATION OF THE APOSTOLIC JOURNEY 120
COVERING, MENTORING & TRAINING IN THE APOSTOLIC ... 127
FIGHTING THE GOOD FIGHT OF FAITH 134
THE WAR LIFE OF AN APOSTLE 155
WARFARE AGAINST IDOLATRY 157
OPERATING IN DREAM & SPIRITUAL REALMS 164
COMBATING TERRITORIAL WARFARE & WITCHCRAFT...167
DEMONIC SPIRITS & WITCHCRAFT THAT ATTACK APOSTLES..172
- Zapping Spirit 172
- Blocking Spirits 172
- Python Spirits 173
- Spirit of Leviathan 173
- Mind Binding & Mind Blinding Spirits 175
- Spirit of Void & Darkness 176

- Spirits of Fear 177
- Spirit of Confusion... 178
- Spirit of the Sluggardness 178
- Spirit of Slander & Accusation.. 179
- Spirits of Affliction & Infirmities..................................... 180
- Spirit of Jezebel 182
- Spirit of Goliath 184
- Spirit of Death & Hell 186

WARFARE DUE TO DIVINE VISIONS & REVELATIONS...189

WARFARE WITH THE SOUL ISSUES OF PEOPLE & MINISTRIES 192

COMBATING RELIGION & TRADITION....................................... 196

EXPOSING SPIRITUAL TRAFFICKING 200

PURPOSE OF ORDINATION 215

APOSTOLIC REFRESHING PRAYER 224

APOSTOLIC DISCIPLINES FOR WELLNESS & REFRESHING........ 226

APOSTOLIC HEALING PRAYER 241

BOOK REFERENCES.. 245

INTRODUCTION INTO APOSTLESHIP

There was a movie released in 2016 that I love called "Dr. Strange." Though the movie is rooted in witchcraft and idolatry of which I do not promote, when I watch it I envision the main character being in Holy Spirit school learning how to operate in spiritual realms and dimensions, and ultimately realizing his true calling – an apostle (yes my spiritual imagination is at work). The main character is a brilliant neurosurgeon named Stephen Strange. He has a horrible accident that severely damages his hands and he can no longer perform surgeries. Devastated and determined to return to his craft – his identity as a neurosurgeon - he seeks alternative healing methods of magic and ancient realities - spiritual gifts and fivefold ministry offices (in my spiritual imagination of course).

In a fight scene, Dr. Strange is SHIFTED into a building with a host of weaponry and artifacts, one that happens to be a mantle. The mantle is alive. YES IT IS ALIVE! Whewwww! Dr.Strange has a gold emblem around his neck that the mantle recognizes. Therefore, the mantle mounts upon him as he is fighting a dark enemy who wants the highest dark power so he can destroy the world. Since the mantle is ALIVE, it literally helps Dr. Strange combat his enemies and protects him during various fight scenes as it directs him on how to maneuver through different challenges. Dr. Strange is still learning magic and how to navigate the alternate realities, so when he is mantled by the powerful red cape, he still does not know what all has come with his new found power and potential. Especially since he is young in this new craft, and is operating in it while at the same time learning about it. He continues to refer to himself as a neurosurgeon and wants to return to his old craft that he is confident and securely skilled in, but unbeknownst to him, his life has SHIFTED into his true calling - his ultimate calling – to which I refer to as an apostle (yes my imagination at work again).

This is how many apostles begin their apostolic careers. We are skilled and intricately successful in our educational career or ministry, then a significant SHIFT takes our lives on an unexpected path. We are thrust into life school with the Holy Spirit to which we embrace because we think it will further equip us in our original craft. We soon realize that an intricate SHIFT has occurred. We cannot go back to the old and do not know how to embrace the new. Holy Spirit school is exciting and the learning is so ravishingly we cannot get enough, yet the comprehension of the realms and dimensions of heaven is intense and the warfare is discombobulating. Just when we think we are clear on what is occurring, our lives embarks upon continual SHIFTS and turns of learning about God and his realities that the average saint has no language or knowledge of. We are thrust into battles with forces unaware. We are not certain on the reason we are fighting, and we are still learning how to use our spiritual weapons to defeat these enemies. As Holy Spirit life school continues, a weight falls upon us. It seems to be alive and has become a part of us. We want to go right, it pulls us left. The mantle is insistent on taking our lives on a destiny pathway with the Lord that we were not initially informed about. A path we eventually submit to and learn to love more than our very own breath. Yet the challenge is, we did not have a say so. We seemed to have no choice like other saints. The choice is made for us, as we did not choose this SHIFT – this calling. The calling is ALIVE with a mind of its own. And its focus is on choosing us.

WELCOME TO THE FOUNDATIONAL TRUTHS OF AN APOSTLE!

SHIFT!

THE APOSTOLIC CALL

The disciples were not given much choice in SHIFTING to apostles either. They were focused on their careers when Jesus passed by and told them to follow him. Jesus called and trained them as disciples, then chose 12 of them to be apostles. They were still learning how to be disciples and to do all the mighty acts Jesus did when they were set a part as apostles. Even with Jesus among them, as they went, they learned how to operate in their apostolic calling. And much of their apostolic calling and work did not manifest until Jesus died on the cross and had ascended to heaven. Though there were foundational similarities, each of their apostolic callings were different and strategically unveiled through their personal identity and relationship with Jesus Christ and the Holy Spirit.

> *Luke 6:13-15* *And when it was day, he called unto him his disciples: and of them he chose twelve, whom also he named apostles; Simon, (whom he also named Peter,) and Andrew his brother, James and John, Philip and Bartholomew, Matthew and Thomas, James the son of Alphaeus, and Simon called Zelotes, And Judas the brother of James, and Judas Iscariot, which also was the traitor.*
>
> *Matthew 10:1-8* *And when he had called unto him his twelve disciples, he gave them power against unclean spirits, to cast them out, and to heal all manner of sickness and all manner of disease. Now the names of the twelve apostles are these; The first, Simon, who is called Peter, and Andrew his brother; James the son of Zebedee, and John his brother; Philip, and Bartholomew; Thomas, and Matthew the*

publican; James the son of Alphaeus, and Lebbaeus, whose surname was Thaddaeus; Simon the Canaanite, and Judas Iscariot, who also betrayed him. These twelve Jesus sent forth, and commanded them, saying, Go not into the way of the Gentiles, and into any city of the Samaritans enter ye not: But go rather to the lost sheep of the house of Israel. And as ye go, preach, saying, The kingdom of heaven is at hand. Heal the sick, cleanse the lepers, raise the dead, cast out devils: freely ye have received, freely give.

Many apostles have a spirit of excellence and border on being perfectionists. Apostles are used to excelling and progressing at accelerated levels, while being clear about who we are, what we embrace, and what we invest in. Many struggle with embracing the call of apostleship because:

- We could not possibly be called to something we have little to no knowledge about
- We could not possibly be called to oversee and govern with minimal initial training
- We are already great at so many other things, how could we possibly be destined to do something that will require the continual extent of our lives to learn and achieve (yes read that one again)
- People do not even embrace this apostolic truth about us so how can it be so
- We had so many friends and supports when we were doing what we were great at, loved and what others loved about us; how could this be our calling if it is such a lonely and misunderstood journey

- How can we be stripped of what we do know then commissioned to learn ourselves and our lives in a different way, yet using the same spirit of excellence and the same but more strategically powerful gifts and talents that we were successful at before hand in a different facet of life

You may ask *"why is this so?" "Why is this necessary?"* Sighhhhhh! I am about to tell you the reason it is so.

When the apostles were set a part, they acknowledged the call and were even obedient in operating in it, but they were not sold out unto death. It was not until Jesus was crucified and rose from the grave that they SHIFTED into operating in the full measure of what it meant to be an apostle.

Apostles is *apostolos* in the Greek and means:

1. a delegate; specially, an ambassador of the Gospel
2. officially a commissioner of Christ ("apostle") (with miraculous powers)
3. apostle, messenger, he that is sent

Dictionary.com defines a *delegate* as:

1. a person designated to act for or represent another or others; deputy; representative, as in a political convention
2. to send or appoint (a person) as deputy or representative
3. to commit (powers, functions, etc.) to another as agent or deputy

Dictionary.com defines *ambassador* as:

1. a diplomatic official of the highest rank, sent by one sovereign or state to another as its resident representative (ambassador extraordinary and plenipotentiary)
2. a diplomatic official of the highest rank sent by a government to represent it on a temporary mission, as for negotiating a treaty
3. an authorized messenger or representative

An apostle is not just a prophetic mouth piece, teacher, proclaimer, or soul winner. Though they operate in all these areas, they are delegates, ambassadors, diplomats, governing officials of Jesus. They are a literal representation of Jesus Christ. They go in his stead to establish and fulfill the work of the kingdom. Just as Jesus went through a process of dying and resurrecting, when an apostle is first called, they too go through a process of dying to self and everything they know about themselves, and when they have fulfilled the process, they rise up in the resurrection calling of an apostle. Once the apostle is resurrected, they do not even care about dying. They forsake any and everything for Jesus Christ, and deem everything they do as unto death.

> **1Corinthians 4:9-14** *For I think that God hath set forth us the apostles last, as it were appointed to death: for we are made a spectacle unto the world, and to angels, and to men. We are fools for Christ's sake, but ye are wise in Christ; we are weak, but ye are strong; ye are honorable, but we are despised. Even unto this present hour we both hunger, and thirst, and are naked, and are buffeted, and have no certain*

dwelling place; And labor, working with our own hands: being reviled, we bless; being persecuted, we suffer it: Being defamed, we entreat: we are made as the filth of the world, and are the offscouring of all things unto this day.

2Corinthians 4:1-2, 7-15 *Therefore seeing we have this ministry, as we have received mercy, we faint not; But have renounced the hidden things of dishonesty, not walking in craftiness, nor handling the word of God deceitfully; but by manifestation of the truth commending ourselves to every man's conscience in the sight of God......But we have this treasure in earthen vessels, that the excellency of the power may be of God, and not of us. We are troubled on every side, yet not distressed; we are perplexed, but not in despair; Persecuted, but not forsaken; cast down, but not destroyed; Always bearing about in the body the dying of the Lord Jesus, that the life also of Jesus might be made manifest in our body. For we which live are alway delivered unto death for Jesus' sake, that the life also of Jesus might be made manifest in our mortal flesh. } So then death works in us, but life in you.*

The stripping process, while receiving hands on training from the Holy Spirit is so all that is not of Jesus dies, and the new you arises in the fullness of his image, identity, character, nature, mindset, and zeal for the kingdom. It is a necessary process to train, equip, and humble you in your destiny. Paul said the apostles were made spectacle, fools, weak, and despised. This is the humility, posture, and lifestyle of the nature of an apostle. It is the same nature Jesus spoke of in

Philippians 2:5-8,

> *Let this mind be in you, which was also in Christ Jesus: Who, being in the form of God, thought it not robbery to be equal with God: But made himself of no reputation, and took upon him the form of a servant, and was made in the likeness of men: And being found in fashion as a man, he humbled himself, and became obedient unto death, even the death of the cross.*

The apostle recognizes that they are actually wise, strong, and honorable, but they dare not yield the impression that they would rob Jesus of any glory as the new resurrected man they have become is only focused on Jesus being exalted and giving glory. The apostle is transformed such that he or she is now capable of yielding God's glory

- in good times and in bad
- when considered fools or wise
- when weak and when strong
- when hungry or full
- when naked or clothed
- when accepted or rejected
- when persecuted or respected
- when troubled and in peace
- when sick or healthy
- in death and life

This is the lifestyle posture God requires of the apostle. He chooses you because he has put it in you to surrender to your calling and destiny. And even though you are stripped of everything you experienced and thought you knew about yourself, all of it was significant and relevant to who you become after you resurrect as an apostle. You will use it all – the career you chose, the education, the positions you held, every gift you possess, every strong character trait, the excellence you operated in, the success and acceleration anointing upon your life, the ability to overcome and persevere, etc. All of it is not in vain. It will give him glory and even more so as it is now mantled in resurrection power.

Exploration Questions & Nuggets:

1. Which stage of your apostolic journey are you in, before resurrection or after resurrection?
2. What has been some of your challenges with embracing the process and all that has come with being in Holy Spirit life school?

3. If you harbor any ill feelings about your calling due to processing, spend time in prayer sharing your thoughts and feelings with the Lord, forgiving him and anyone else that you are challenged with; ask him to heal you of any wounds you may have.
4. What are your thoughts and feelings regarding the revelation of being God's representative – a literal representation - prototype of him?
5. What needs to die in you so you can fully surrender and resurrect into apostleship?
6. If you have already resurrected, spend time journaling about your experience. Explore whether you have the nature of Jesus Christ where he receives glory from your life no matter the season you are in.
7. If this is not your testimony, search out with the Holy Spirit areas you need deliverance and healing where you are sold out unto death. Revisit your life posture from time to time with the Holy Spirit so you live in this stance of humility unto Jesus.

GOD ORCHESTRATES THE CALL

I am founder and overseer of Kingdom Shifters Ministries in Muncie, Indiana. I am also founder of Kingdom Wellness Counseling and Mentoring Center and Kingdom Shifters Christian Empowerment Center. Kingdom Shifters Ministries (KSM) is a Jesus focused fivefold ministry with a heart to see people, churches, and communities, healed, delivered, and liberated to walk in the fullness of their destiny. KSM uses various ministry styles, businesses, organizations, and marketplace outlets to shift people and atmospheres out of darkness and into the light of God.

At the beginning of 2013, I transitioned out of a church I had been a member and leader of for 12 years. Before I left, I had already launched and been operating through KSM for two and a half years. Though I was active with teaching, ministering, and assisting ministries and the church with various endeavors, I had stepped down from leading any particular ministry as I was focused on KSM. The Lord told me to start hosting monthly Holy Ghost Agenda Miracles Services in my home town and that eventually KSM would be its own entity. He told me to transition out of my church and that he would bring me nontraditional covering to oversee my ministry. At the time I did not know what this entailed, but I was obedient.

Though I had transitioned correctly by engaging in several meetings with my pastors before leaving, sharing the heart and vision God had given me with my them and those close to me at the church and abroad, setting deadlines for conversations and meetings and a leaving date, saying a formal "goodbye" and blessing to the congregation, transitioning still had its challenges. Though I was excited and embracing of the new, it was a very lonely, hurtful, and confusing season as:

- Many I thought supported me did not
- Many who I thought understood my transition did not
- Many who initially blessed it, later cursed it
- Many mistook my transition and obedience to God as abandonment and thus betrayed and scorned me
- Many supported me in secret but shunned and gossiped about me in public
- Many did not recognize that though I was leaving the church I was not backsliding or rebelling; I was simply extending the kingdom

Despite it all, I had a work to do and I was determined to do it healthy and unoffended. I would therefore lay on my face day after day, sometimes several times a day, releasing my pain, betrayal, confusion, my sense of loss, grief, and loneliness to God. I also increased my reading on the apostolic and anything related to my calling. I began reading a book entitled *"Spurned Into Apostleship,"* by Apostle Jackie Green of Redlands, California. As I towered through the pages, it was like reading my life's story. I had temporary covering during this time. I knew I needed mentoring and assistance in my apostolic calling and in how to shift forward in what God was telling me. I had no idea where I was going to get that from as my temporary covering was more so for accountability purposes and to save face because as people and ministries heard about my transition, they began to speak curses that I was out of order and would fail due to not having covering. Yet, God said he was going to send proper covering, so I just held on to that, and kept shifting forward in what he would lead me in doing.

I will admit that I did not have all the answers when I transitioned out of my old church. I remember my pastors asking me questions and stating, "*I do not know, but when God tells me I will surely tell you.*" I had to be at peace with the unknown and not allow it to instill fear in me or stifle me from doing what I was clear on God telling me to do. Sometimes we do not know the full plan and we use this as an excuse not to SHIFT, even though the SHIFT is necessary and detrimental if we are disobedient. I will admit that if I knew the full plan at the time, I probably would have hesitated with leaving. I would have battled increased internal and external warfare, as I would have felt even more inadequate and people would have been all the more challenged with my transition. I was obedient to what God did share at the time and even after leaving the church, I would share answers with the my previous pastors as my journey unfolded.

On a Sunday in March of 2013, I was reading from *Spurned Into Apostleship,* and the Lord told me to look on the back of the book and contact the author. I was like "*What?*" I began to go back and forth with the Lord, telling him that no one contacts an author. But he insisted, so I looked and found an email address. I told the Lord I would email on Monday and he was like *"right now."* I was like *"no one checks their ministry email on Sunday."* And he was every adamant in me emailing in that moment, so I reluctantly sent an email expressing that I was an upcoming apostle and desired mentoring in my calling. I shared a few other things and abruptly ended the email with something to the fact that *"if this is a divine connection then I look forward to hearing from you."*

Not even five minutes later my phone rang and I did not recognize the number, but I knew it was a response to my email. God kept telling me to answer the phone but I just stared at it. I finally answered and the voice asked for Taquetta Baker. I was shocked because most folks tear my name up. But she pronounced it correctly. She introduced herself as Prophet Cathy and that she was Apostle Green's Armorbearer. By my responses, she could tell I was in shock. She asked was I ok and I said that I was not expecting anyone to be answering their email on a Sunday morning. She expressed that she was preparing to minister at the Sunday service but God told her to check the ministries email. She told the Lord that she does not check emails on Sunday and that she needed to finish her sermon. God told her that she was trying to minister to who she wanted to, but he was trying to get her to minister to who he wanted her to minister to. She said after that rebuke she checked the email account, saw my email and immediately called Apostle Green. Apostle Green had also checked the email at the leading of the Lord and was about to call Prophet Cathy and tell her to call me. Prophet Cathy prayed and encouraged me and told me Apostle Green would contact me in a couple of days. A couple days later Apostle Green contacted me and we have been connected since that day. I joined the AIM - Apostle In The Making Mentoring Program - and eventually KSM became an affiliate ministry under JGM Enternational Prayerlife Institute. AIM - Apostles in the Making Program is a personalized mentoring program for

- Apostles that are emerging into their apostleship.
- Apostles that are already functioning but need to be connected to an apostolic mentor and network.
- Apostles that are just discovering who they are and need to be birthed into their apostleship through prayer and personal mentorship of an apostolic parent.

When I first met Apostle Green she had prayed and searched God about who I was, and had a tailor made vision plan for my apostolic mentoring journey that would allow me to be delivered, healed, defined, clarified, confirmed, set, ordained, and released into my calling. And I received a pile of books and CD's that only increased as the journey progressed. I received additional books via email, and every time Apostle Green would write a book during the time I was being initially trained and prepared for ordination, she would tell me to read it and complete a paper on EACH chapter of the book. The work load was greater than when I was pursuing my Master's degree in Counseling at the University of Missouri Saint Louis. I kept saying I expect to get a doctorate after all this work, especially since after ordination, I continued to read any book Apostle Green would write and believe me it's a host of them. I even sent the picture below declaring an honorary doctorate.

Apostle Green has since launched an online and satellite Christian University called Rapha Deliverance

University. I will be acquiring a doctorate in 2018. Of course I have a whole other vision plan to complete. But it is so worth it, and so is embracing and journeying in my call as an apostle.

Exploration Questions & Nuggets:

1. What is God encouraging and requiring of you in this season of your life?
2. What is hindering you from embracing and SHIFTING into being obedient to what God is saying?
3. What do you have to do or need to do to SHIFT with God?
4. Spend time releasing those hinderances and relinquish them to God, and ask him to give you peace about the decisions you have to make in this season.

5. Set a deadline commitment to have the necessary conversations and make the necessary moves to shift with God. Stick to your deadline and have a responsible person hold you accountable and that can intercede for you as you close chapters of your old season and embrace your new.
6. After the conversations and meetings, move forward with trusting God, while being in open expectation of new connections, relationships, mentoring, guidance, covering, and whatever else is needed for a successful journey.
7. As you SHIFT remain close to God as it will be lonely at times and you will feel grieved due to what you had to relinquish. Share your thoughts, feelings, fears, and frustrations continually with God so he can cleanse you, heal you, and further guide you in embracing and staying in the momentum of the **SHIFT!**

FOUNDATION & RELEVANCY

Of APOSTLESHIP

Ephesians 4:11-16 *And he gave some, apostles; and some, prophets; and some, evangelists; and some, pastors and teachers; For the perfecting of the saints, for the work of the ministry, for the edifying of the body of Christ: Till we all come in the unity of the faith, and of the knowledge of the Son of God, unto a perfect man, unto the measure of the stature of the fulness of Christ: That we henceforth be no more children, tossed to and fro, and carried about with every wind of doctrine, by the sleight of men, and cunning craftiness, whereby they lie in wait to deceive; But speaking the truth in love, may grow up into him in all things, which is the head, even Christ: From whom the whole body fitly joined together and compacted by that which every joint supplieth, according to the effectual working in the measure of every part, maketh increase of the body unto the edifying of itself in love.*

It is important to note that there are not any scriptures in the Bible stating that once Jesus gave these fivefold ministry offices as gifts to the church, we can pick and choose whether to use them or not and decide when they are no longer relevant. When Jesus gives us gifts they are needful and necessary. Even though we are equipped with all types of gifts and we choose which gifts we want to operate in and flourish in, we do not get to reject the others as irrelevant if we do not want them. We are still responsible for those gifts, and still have to respect those gifts in others.

It has been man and man's doctrine that has decided which office gifts they would embrace and utilize, and which ones they would reject and kill. Jesus knows what we have need of and knows what will bless us with sufficiently walking in destiny and building up his church. This is the reason we are one body with different members. We are not required to do it all, but we are required to work together to see the whole body fully operable and healthy (*1Corinthians 12:12-27*).

<u>Perfection</u> is *katartismos* in the Greek and means:
1. complete furnishing (objectively)
2. perfecting, equipping

Since these gifts are given for the perfecting of the saints and the church, when we reject them, we

- Reject being sufficiently furnished in our ability to build, train, and equip quality saints that can walk in the fullness of salvation, adequately proclaim the gospel, and save souls for Jesus Christ.
- Reject the identity and destiny of those who have been called to operate in these particular offices; thus these saints are left questioning, wandering, and stifled in their identity and calling. They end up being mediocre church members, bound to religious works that do not impact the community or the world, or backsliders tossed between the church and the world or God and doctrine.
- We reject being perfected saints and ministries that can effectively impact and be key catalysts within the communities and regions we are apart of.
- We reject being able to operate as spiritual governors and rulers within the world. We were designed to have fruitful dominion in the earth per

Genesis 1:28, but at this point we are just trying to remain relevant. We have rejected the very gifts that would have given us sufficient dominion in the earth.

> *Genesis 1:28 And God blessed them, and God said unto them, Be fruitful, and multiply, and replenish the earth, and subdue it: and have dominion over the fish of the sea, and over the fowl of the air, and over every living thing that moveth upon the earth.*

Though it may appear as a spiritual awakening to us, the movement that we see today where the apostles and prophets are rising up, is not
- A new fad
- A demonic rebellion against or within people and the church
- A new concept God is implementing in the earth

We see that clearly from Ephesians 4. This is an equipping Jesus gave to the church. We have failed to govern and utilize it to effectively empower our ministries and the world. I believe the uprising we are experiencing is due to saints really pursuing a relationship with God for themselves - really seeking to know who they are in the earth and who he is in them. As God reveals to some that they are apostles and prophets, they are rebelling against

- Self-rejection of their identity and calling
- Religious and doctrinal rejection of their identity and calling
- Accepting who God says they are with commitment to walk in it and see his will come to pass in the earth

What appears to be a new movement is just personal spiritual awakening - a divine revolution of suppressed identities and callings. People are no longer allowing the church who lacks vision of who they are, and even of who it is to define them. They are seeking God for definition and identity. And those who have developed a hate for the church are defining themselves (which is dangerous).

Anytime you have righteous rebellion that presents as a divine revolution, the enemy will seek to use those who are insecure and lost in their identity and calling to contaminate and instill fear where the church and the world will not want to embrace those who are truly called to these offices. Thus, you have a whole bunch of people claiming to be apostles and prophets without the true fruit, character and integrity, or mantle of the calling.

- This however, is not a reason to further reject the offices. If anything, it reveals the importance of identifying the genuine apostles and prophets, and equipping them so that they can show forth the fruit and significance of such gifts to the church and the world.

Apostles have always been relevant - in the Bible days and even today.

- If you study the doctrine, the main premises for not believing there are apostles today is that these oracles believe apostles physically walked with Jesus and could provide an eye witnessing account of his life and workings. (Scriptures Study: *Acts 1:25-26, Acts 5:32,*

Luke 1:1-4, 1Corinthians 9:1, 1Corinthians 15:8, 2Peter 1:12). If you study the scriptures you will realize that the apostles would make reference to walking with Jesus because they did not want to deny, reject or shun him as they did when he was being crucified. They also understood that giving eye witness accounts was essential to people believing them and receiving salvation. Before Jesus ascended he promised to send his Holy Spirit that would teach us all things concerning him. Moreover, Jesus told the apostles to testify of their relationship and journey with him.

> *John 14:26 But the Comforter, which is the Holy Ghost, whom the Father will send in my name, he shall teach you all things, and bring all things to your remembrance, whatsoever I have said unto you.*
>
> *John 15:25-26 But when the Comforter is come, whom I will send unto you from the Father, even the Spirit of truth, which proceedeth from the Father, he shall testify of me: And ye also shall bear witness, because ye have been with me from the beginning.*

Jesus encouraged them to share their testimony as it would be confirmation of what the Holy Spirit would reveal to people. Jesus also clearly explained that he was sending the Holy Spirit to dwell in us, and to teach us all things about him as we are guided in our destiny journey. Therefore, to build a premise that apostles are no longer among us because Jesus is not physically here walking with us in human form is crazy. The Holy Spirit, Jesus presence, is living in us and journeying with us daily. To deem apostles as irrelevant today is to say that we do not need or do not have the Holy Spirit dwelling among and in us, that the Holy Spirit is not capable of teaching us about Jesus, equipping us in the identity, character, nature, and calling of Jesus, or able to aid us in building up the church. It is not doctrinally sound and is an erred use of scripture.

- Another premise that attempts to deem apostles irrelevant today is the concept that the foundation of the church is already laid.

> *1Corinthians 3:10-13* *According to the grace of God which is given unto me, as a wise masterbuilder, I have laid the foundation, and another buildeth thereon. But let every man take heed how he buildeth thereupon. For other foundation can no man lay than that is laid, which is Jesus Christ. Now if any man build upon this foundation gold, silver, precious stones, wood, hay, stubble; Every man's work shall be made manifest: for the day shall declare it, because it shall be revealed by fire; and the fire shall try every man's work of what sort it is. If any man's work abide which he hath built thereupon, he shall receive a reward. If any man's work shall be burned, he shall suffer loss: but he himself shall be saved; yet so as by fire.*

Though apostles lay foundation, they are not trying to change Jesus as the foundation, or change the initial foundation of the church. Even Paul said, there is one foundation which is Jesus Christ. The foundation Paul laid was Jesus Christ, and he was letting the people know that no other idolatrous foundation should be laid. Apostles lay the foundation of Jesus and govern the foundations of Jesus that has been laid by other builders, while making sure what is being built has a biblical and healthy foundation that is rooted in the truth of who Jesus Christ is. The foundations of the works built upon Jesus Christ, the chief founder and rock of our salvation does require the work of the apostle. The apostle has the blueprint and is efficient in making sure the foundation is biblical, has God's heart and blessing, and it eternally solid. Apostles were necessary in the Bible times, and still are today.

> ***The Message Bible Verse 10-13*** *Using the gift God gave me as a good architect, I designed blueprints; Apollos is putting up the walls. Let each carpenter who comes on the job take care to build on the foundation! Remember, there is only one foundation, the one already laid: Jesus Christ. Take particular care in picking out your building materials. Eventually there is going to be an inspection. If you use cheap or inferior materials, you'll be found out.*

Many pastors have tried to do the work of apostles and now many churches have a faulty foundation. Clear vision was not utilized to sufficiently build a solid foundation that had Jesus Christ's word, character, nature, standards, vision, and blueprint. Many pastors build works on passion, doctrine, and biblical formulas. But the works of Jesus Christ must be clear, strategic, and solid as a rock.

> ***Ephesians 2:19-21*** *Now therefore ye are no more strangers and foreigners, but fellow citizens with the saints, and of the household of God; And are built upon the foundation of the apostles and prophets, Jesus Christ himself being the chief corner stone; In whom all the*

> building fitly framed together groweth unto an holy temple in the Lord: In whom ye also are builded together for an habitation of God through the Spirit.
>
> **Matthew 16:18** And I say also unto thee, That thou art Peter, and upon this rock I will build my church; and the gates of hell shall not prevail against it.

Passion is great, but it is mostly emotional and birthed in the heart, with minimal spiritual direction necessary for the foundation to sustain through testing and trials, and throughout generations. The pastor also tends to do much of the work. Most builders have a team working with them. When Jesus gave the church fivefold ministry gifts in Ephesians 4, he equipped us with a team for the work of the ministry. When the disciples ministered, they went out as a team. When the apostles ministered, they operated as a team. The apostle is not going to steal the passion of the pastor or take the position of the pastor. The apostle will join in the work, help bring vision and clarity to the work God is giving the pastor, provide a blueprint so it has a solid foundation, and journey with the pastor as he continues to build upon the part of Jesus Christ that has been governed to his or her hands.

Apostolic Prayer: Decreeing an awakening of spiritual enlightenment is coming to you even now to embrace the apostle and even the prophet as apart of your foundational team. Decreeing that pastors, teachers, and evangelists realize that you need the apostle and the prophet and that they discern that they need you. We are innately joined together as governmental gifts to the body of Christ and the world. Decreeing we all understand that we are ill-equipped without one another. Decreeing we desire to be a team and pursue the team we are to be apart of to sufficiently establish and build up God's kingdom. **SHIFT!**

CHARACTERISTICS OF AN APOSTLE

A Holy principality
Righteous
Pure
Patient
Unconditionally loving
Peaceful
Meek
Steadfastness
Constant
Consistent
Persistent
Determined
Enduring
Deliberate
An overcomer
Makes the difficult look easy
Purposeful
Loyal
Integral
Forgiving
Trustworthy
Discerning
Faithful
Unwavering
Fearless
Bold
Radical
Confident
Unique
Extremely peculiar
Misunderstood
Zealous leader
Supernatural
Miracle worker
A Sign & a wonder
Do mighty exploits
Deliverer
Healer
Transformer
Shifter/Shaker
Change Agent
Curse breaker
Demon buster
A walking bible
Access to kingdom
Mysteries & revelation
Rooted & grounded in Jesus
Cocky about the gospel of Jesus
Defends the gospel
Confrontational
Raw preacher
Fearless teacher
Minister of sound doctrine
Compassionate for souls
Sold out
Self sacrificed
Dead to self & worldly things
Quick to fast & consecrate
Glory carrier
Full of power
Friend of God
Friend of the Holy Spirit
Ambassador of Jesus
Has angelic help
Relevant
Current
Timely
Punctual

- Fruitful
- Successful
- Humble
- Intense
- Mothering
- Fathering
- Protector
- Mentor
- Counselor
- Coach
- Trainer
- Equipper
- Disciple maker
- Governor
- Administrator
- Serious
- Focused
- Disciplined
- Observant
- Intolerable to ignorance, unholiness, laziness
- Adaptive to change
- Introverted
- Extroverted when necessary
- Consistent communing with Jesus
- Stern
- Influential
- Strategic
- Honest
- Honoring
- Persuasive
- Forthright
- Extremely wise
- Years ahead of self & others
- Educated
- Extremely Intelligent
- Knowledgeable
- Witty
- Creative/witty ideas
- Multifaceted
- Generator of wealth
- Supernaturally blessed
- Favor with God & men
- Multi-tasker
- Scribe
- Gifted
- Uses the foolish to confound the prideful/wise
- Helpful
- Planter/lays foundations
- Plower
- Builder
- Harvester
- Establisher
- Infiltrator
- Uprooter
- Judge/releases throne room judgment
- Just
- Problem solver
- Orderly
- Sets order
- Gathers & unifies
- Causes uprisings & riots to the demonic & evil matters
- Revolutionist
- Reformer
- Perfecter of people
- Spirit of excellence
- Teachable
- Life learner

- Dreams & Visions
- Visionary
- Forerunner
- Pioneer
- Trailblazer
- Foresighted
- Atmospheric
- Governor of multiple realms
- Raising of the dead
- Raising dead dreams & visions
- Years ahead of most people
- Generational focused
- Kingdom focused
- Nationally focused
- Prophetic
- Warrior
- Prayer warrior
- A weapon of destruction
- Battle ready
- Career of Warfare
- Confronts Witches & Warlocks
- Intercessory
- Watchman/Watcher
- Gatekeeper
- A Key/Pathway Opener
- Praiser
- Worshipper

THIS IS WHO YOU ARE APOSTLE & MORE! YOU ARE AN ETERNAL WORK THAT IS CONSTANTLY UNVEILING FOR GOD'S GLORY! ENJOY, EMBRACE, BECOME & JOY IN WHO YOU ARE! IT IS AN IDENTITY & JOURNEY OF CAPTIVATION & FRUITFULNESS! IT IS YOU!
SHIFT!

NATURE OF AN APOSTLE

Though apostles will operate through different wells of anointing, possess unique mantles, exude strong manifestations in the other offices listed in *Ephesians 4:11*, flow in and out of the spiritual gifts in *1Corinthians 12*, the key signs of an apostle are as followed:

- Special relationship with Jesus Christ and the Holy Spirit
- Personal commissioning of being called and sent by Jesus Christ
- Inducted into Holy Spirit life school where they are called, equipped, trained, confirmed, and utilized as an apostle
- Innate ability to pioneer and trail blaze ideas, movements, works, ministries, businesses
- Effective with equipping and training people and ministries in biblical and specialized areas
- Strong deliverance, healing, SHIFTING, and breakthrough anointing
- Miracles, signs, and wonders following his or her works
- They bring increase to God's kingdom and fruit to people, ministries, works, and whatever is governed by their hands
- Skilled on bringing alignment (order) to people, ministries, and regions
- Unexplainable ability to persevere and overcome adversity
- Skilled in identifying, mentoring and raising up leaders that can carry and train others to fulfill

the work of the Lord
- Live a life of complete sacrifice and death unto the Lord and his kingdom

Apostles do not just plant and establish churches. Church planting may be a part of what some apostles do, but is not all of what apostles do. Apostles plant and establish works in the lives of people, families, ministries, communities, regions, nations, businesses, organizations, the marketplace, political arenas, and within the world system. The foundation of an apostle is to displace and dismantle darkness, falsehoods, immorality, idolatries, demonic structures, mindsets & kingdoms, while establishing, building up, and advancing the kingdom of God in the earth. Even as we have a lot of chatter in the body of Christ about taking worldly mountains, please know **APOSTLE**, that God is not looking to take over darkness and dark kingdoms. He does not want Hollywood, the evil dealings of marketplace businesses, political agencies, the public educational systems, etc. Though we can have impact in these areas, God's will is to establish his own kingdom and to replace idolatrous kingdoms. While we are wasting our time trying to overtake the devil's systems, we should be building and establishing our own. This is the foundational nature, focus, and work of an apostle.

2Corinthians 10:4-6 *(For the weapons of our warfare are not carnal, but mighty through God to the pulling down of strong holds;) Casting down imaginations, and every high thing that exalteth itself against the knowledge of God, and bringing into captivity every thought to the obedience of Christ; And having in a readiness to revenge all disobedience, when your obedience is fulfilled.*

The Amplified Bible *For the weapons of our warfare are not physical [weapons of flesh and blood], but they are mighty before God for the overthrow and destruction of strongholds, [Inasmuch as we] refute arguments and theories and reasonings and every proud and lofty thing that sets itself up against the [true] knowledge of God; and we lead every thought and purpose away captive into the obedience of Christ (the Messiah, the Anointed One), being in readiness to punish every [insubordinate for his] disobedience, when your own submission and obedience [as a church] are fully secured and complete.*

The Message Bible *The tools of our trade aren't for marketing or manipulation, but they are for demolishing that entire massively corrupt culture. We use our powerful God-tools for smashing warped philosophies, tearing down barriers erected against the truth of God, fitting every loose thought and emotion and impulse into the structure of life shaped by Christ. Our tools are ready at hand for clearing the ground of every obstruction and building lives of obedience into maturity.*

When apostles are allowed to operate in their calling, SHIFTS, transformation, revealing of God's kingdom and plan, and eternal success is evident. Apostles SHIFT people, ministries, businesses, organizations, communities, regions, nations into the will, plan, and alignment of the Lord. Through these SHIFTS, transformation occurs, as anything that is not like God is exposed, refuted, and dealt with (uprooted, torn down, destroyed and overthrown). And anything that is of God is identified, built up, planted, plowed, watered, produced, and reproduced, to bring continual increase.

> *Jeremiah 1:10* See, I have this day set thee over the nations and over the kingdoms, to root out, and to pull down, and to destroy, and to throw down, to build, and to plant.

Though this is also the work of the prophet's anointing that rests upon the apostle, they also have the responsibility that as things are SHIFTED and transformed, they are given vision plans to help govern the SHIFT and transformation, such that God's will is evident and sustaining no matter what the devil, godless people, and governments do in the earth.

The work of an apostle is so intricate that even if that work was just for a season, its effects and establishment has eternal impact. We see this with every apostle in the Bible, even Judas the betrayer. Even though he committed suicide - destroying his life and destiny - his apostolic impact has had eternal effects upon people, the church, the world, and the generations.

Even as the apostolic is the foundation of every believer, apostles have the grace, power, and ability to gather people so that kingdom structure, training, equipping, anointing, and miracles, signs and wonders can be stirred and imparted where people can be used for God's glory. Apostles help bring administrative and governmental order to churches, ministries, businesses, organizations, specific works, people, communities, regions, and nations. Sometimes when we hear the word "*order*" we shun it and we shun apostles. We equate order with people telling us what to do. We rather remain chaotic, disorganized, cycling, stifled, and misaligned with God and the things of God, than to receive order - than to embrace apostles. How intelligent is that concept?

Apostles are not designed or called to dictate to you, boss you around, or takeover your position or platform. They are gifted with the ability to receive a vision plan and strategy from God on how people, churches, ministries, businesses, organizations, specific works, communities, regions, and nations operate. They also organize, teach, equip, administrate, and oversee others in working that plan and vision, such that they successfully progress in establishing God's will in the earth.

Apostolic Order Produces:
- The character and nature of God
- The will, plan, kingdom, glory, and favor of God
- Power, comfort & instruction of the Holy Spirit
- Alignment/Set order/Straighten the crooked & false
- Balance
- Exposure
- Truth
- Judgment of the unhealthy & the demonic
- Deliverance
- Healing

- Breakthrough
- Freedom
- Healthiness & wellness
- Proper government & rulership
- Establishes the kingdom of God
- Liberty in the Holy Spirit
- Open heavens
- Kingdom empowerment
- Subduing of destiny
- Dominion
- Productivity
- Reproduction
- Consistency
- Sustaining success
- Clear vision to further progress successfully

If you want the will of God in your life, ministry, business, and region, then you must embrace and deem order as a blessing and necessity to your kingdom walk. It is important to embrace apostles, and to recognize that God has given them the humility to establish order without abusing you or the authority that is on their lives.

> **Titus 1:5** *For this cause left I thee in Crete, that thou shouldest set in order the things that are wanting, and ordain elders in every city, as I had appointed thee:*
>
> **The Amplified** *Bible For this reason I left you [behind] in Crete, that you might set right what was defective and finish what was left undone, and that you might appoint elders and set them over the churches (assemblies) in every city as I directed you.*

Apostles are key to identifying and confirming the calling of others and helping them to seek God for a strategic vision plan to walking successfully in their calling and destiny. In *1Timothy 1*, we see Paul embracing and confirming the call on Timothy's life and giving Timothy a clear vision plan so that he may endure warfare and live faithful to the things of God.

Some apostles have a specific remnant they are to personally mother/father, and/or mentor. Apostles will raise up this remnant so that the future generation can be equipped to carry on the kingdom of God.

Apostles are future focused, generational focused, and operate in a global mindset. They are about establishing an eternal work that sustains families, generations, communities, regions, and the world at large. The vision plan they receive will produce necessary now fruit, while focused on generating multiplied consistent fruit that will sustain until Jesus comes. Notice I said "necessary now fruit." This is where apostles and other leaders/saints bump heads. The apostle will not be focused on:

- Quick get rich schemes
- Quick hustles
- Feeding the flesh or validating egos
- Fanfare
- Building platforms and high positions
- Filling up pews for the sake of numbers
- Using gimmicks, mixture, or ungodly tactics to flatter or progress

Apostles appear intimidating and serious and though confident, firm, and forthright, are very loving and humble. The intimidation and seriousness is due to being innately focused on the things of the Lord and pleasing the Lord. There heart is not to make you inferior as this is simply a part of their genetic code.

Apostles are mapping out your vision plan and calling in the spirit, while you are sharing your day to day challenges and woes. It is not that they are not interested in your issues. They see all of you through the eyes of God, and are designed to not only put out fires, but make sure the fire never burns again, as they seek to SHIFT you into destiny alignment.

Apostles are rooted in the principles and standards of God. They will preach, teach, exude, and live holiness or hell. For this very reason, their very presentation may offend some and intimidate others, as their very lifestyles are used to judge sin and ungodliness. Without opening their mouths, their lives will demonstrate and declare the very character, nature, heart, and will of God. Those who are resistant to holiness will be offended or challenged by the very existence of the apostle. They will seek to prove that the apostle is not as holy as he or she presents, even to the point of provoking drama and conflict to render the apostle to sin, character flaws, and discrepancies.

Apostles operate with a sense of urgency. Not that they are trying to control you and rush you. I dare not say apostles will not push you or provoke you, as apostles have an innate urgency to see you be exactly who God designed you to be. To apostles, wasting time is a sin. Apostles are actually grieved when their time is wasted doing pointless unfruitful, unproductive things. Apostles have such a mandate on their lives that they live as if every second counts. Every opportunity matters. Every experience is important. Every encounter is significant to what they are to be doing in the earth and who God is in the earth realm. So please forgive the apostle if they do not sit around *"shooting the breeze,"* do not engage in the mundane, is easily bored, not entertained by worldliness, not interested in the mediocre, unfruitful, or the temporary, invests in real potential and not perceived potential, always appear to be living in and through their Bible and dialoging with and about Jesus. It is not their heart to negate, overlook, pressure, offend, or cause you to feel inferior. It is their identity and calling to invest in that which is ready for the mantle that is on their lives.

Apostles operate in a spirit of excellence which sometimes borders on perfectionism. Apostles have an innate drive for:
- Order and alignment
- Neatness/things being in their precise place
- Cleanliness
- Flawlessness
- For achievement and setting a high performance standard for success
- Excelling at everything they put their hands to

These attributes tend to be accompanied by critical self-evaluations and wanting to please and obey God at all cost. People who work with apostles can find this intimidating and pressuring. Though the apostle is requiring excellence, many tend to feel challenged to achieve the expectations of living by Godly standards of wellness and integrity, especially if they are not ready to rid their lives of sin, or enter the process to be fully delivered and healed. This can also be challenging if the apostle has not submitted their perfectionistic quality to God, where it is cultivated into spiritual excellence. When operating in perfectionism versus a spirit of excellence, the apostle:

- Is striving and working through their own strength rather than the strength of God and the mantle that is on their lives
- Imposes unrealistic demands on self and others that are impossible to obtain
- Create unrealistic standards on themselves because they have no concept of healthy development with time, practice, and study
- Focused on excelling rather than processing with God
- Serve their ambition rather than God's vision
- Place undo pressure upon themselves to perform and excel, which causes stress, burdens, and afflictions
- Mistake unnecessary burdens as the weight of their mantle; they then become bewitched into believing that their will and standards are God's will and standards
- Yield to fear as the apostle think God is challenged with them when they do not live up to their self imposed expectations. It is not God who is challenged with the apostle, it is the apostle's own soul operating against their identity, while succumbing to condemnation, shame and guilt, and inferiority due to not meeting their own unrealistic expectations
- Is being formed in the image of their personal perception of what perfection is,

- rather than the image of God
- Focuses on running away from failure rather than resting in the place of excellence in God, where success is inevitable
- Aims to attain a false reality of perfection rather than the truth of the mantle and who God created us to be
- Risk destroying the God identity and destiny of others as they are focused on meeting their will and standards rather than God's standards

The bible does not tell us to be perfect as God is the one that can perfect those things which concerns us (**Psalms 138:8**). The bible does tell us to operate in a spirit of excellence. It is important for the apostle to know that they do not have to be perfectionistic or strive for perfection as excellence is a part of their nature. It is who they are.

> ***Daniel 5:12*** *Forasmuch as an excellent spirit, and knowledge, and understanding, interpreting of dreams, and shewing of hard sentences, and dissolving of doubts, were found in the same Daniel, whom the king named Belteshazzar: now let Daniel be called, and he will shew the interpretation.*

> ***Daniel 6:3*** *This Daniel was preferred above the presidents and princes, because an excellent spirit was in him; and the king thought to set him over the whole realm.*

<u>*Excellent* is *yatiyr* in the Hebrew and means:</u>
1. preeminent; as an adverb, very: — exceeding, excellent
2. pre-eminent (superior, distinguished, towering), surpassing, extreme
3. extraordinary, exceedingly, extremely

<u>Dictionary.com defines *excellent* as:</u>
1. possessing outstanding quality or superior merit; remarkably good
2. Archaic. extraordinary; superior

When apostles operate in excellence, the excellency of God prevails in their lives and calling, in peoples lives, families, generations, ministries, businesses, the marketplace, communities, regions, and nations. Just as saints should embrace order, we should embrace the spirit of excellence. Through the spirit of excellence, apostles help saints to operate in and display the heart, character, and nature of God so that people are drawn unto salvation, while wanting to live an eternal walk with him.

Apostles need lots of time with Jesus. Most of them prefer time with Jesus, the presence of the Holy Spirit, their bible, and with working on the vision and plans Jesus has granted to their hands, as opposed to fellowshipping with people or engaging in mundane things.

Most apostles have a ravenous spirit for Jesus. Often the apostle will feel empty when they are really full. They are insatiable. They continually crave and hunger for the word, will, and presence of Jesus and is always seeking to have more of him. Only the authentic encounters with Jesus can fulfill the apostle. They will be grieved by false encounters, witchcraft encounters, and encounters that do not reveal the full will or breakthrough of Jesus.

Holy Spirit tends to be the best friend of an apostle. This can be difficult to embrace at first as apostles will want tangible supports that can identify with them, understand them, encourage them, and SHIFT continually with them. Though the apostle will have a specified small support system, that support system will sympathize with them and encourage who they are and what they are doing, but there will always be a void that only the Holy Spirit will be able to fill. The apostle will not initially understand that their genetic spiritual make up is to rely on the Holy Spirit, constantly commune with him, and engage him as their ultimate friend. This is learned as time in Holy Spirit life school becomes the lifestyle of the apostle, and they realize that even as they would want supports and understanding, their greatest joy is getting to know, residing inside, and communing with the Holy Spirit.

Mates, family members, friends, and ministry affiliates will need to respect the nature and character of an apostle. They will have to be okay with Jesus being the head, center, core, and yearning of the apostle's life; and that time with Holy Spirit is essential to the spiritual and natural wealth and health of the apostle. Loved ones must also understand that this does not negate their position in the apostle's life. The apostle needs them and loves them dearly. Their love for God does not replace their love for them.

The apostle will have to be cognizant of the needs and desires of their mates, family members, friends, and ministry affiliates. They will have to be effective - consistent communicators, and heart felt expressers of their love, devotion, and appreciation for those in their life. Despite not having a love for the mundane, the apostle will have to allow their love for their marriage, family, friends, etc., empower them to take time to nurture, cultivate, and strengthen relationships, and to even view this as important to God for their life.

I will state that regardless to how much time the apostle spends with family and friends, because of the call upon the apostle's life and the need for communing with the Holy Spirit, there is a huge sacrifice regarding time and relationships, that the apostle and his or her loved ones have to endure. The calling of the apostle costs and I am not sure there is anyway around that. I do know that Jesus himself said that a hundredfold return will come to those who sacrifice in this nature. I therefore, hold on to that and pray that my family and friends can love me through my calling, and respect that Jesus will bless us for all the sacrifices we endeavor for him and his kingdom.

> **Mark 10:29-31** *Then Peter began to say unto him, Lo, we have left all, and have followed thee. And Jesus answered and said, Verily I say unto you, There is no man that hath left house, or brethren, or sisters, or father, or mother, or wife, or children, or lands, for my sake, and the gospel's, But he shall receive an*

> *hundredfold now in this time, houses, and brethren, and sisters, and mothers, and children, and lands, with persecutions; and in the world to come eternal life. But many that are first shall be last; and the last first.*

Apostles experience seasons of loneliness and isolation. This can and may very well be abandonment as some will leave for legitimate reasons, some leave because it is God's design, some will leave for stupid reasons, and some will leave for no apparent reason at all. Sometimes having to spend time with the Holy Spirit can in and of itself, cause loneliness and abandonment. People feel unappreciated and ostracized by the apostle's time with the Holy Spirit so they leave or they may not understand the call and requirements of an apostle, so they leave. Some just simply cannot go where God is taking the apostle so the isolation with the Holy Spirit causes a separation.

Though the ministry, community, or business endeavors can be full of people or the home of an apostle can be full of family, the apostle can still experience loneliness and isolation. The apostle is often years ahead of those around them, so while others are engaged in the present vision, they are with God working on visions that are ten to twenty years into the future. This can be lonely and boring when the apostle is not able to share what God is speaking or if those around them are not ready to hear or engage in future visions. The apostle has to practice finding joy in watching others blossom and in seeing visions unfold in the present, even when they have already lived the vision in their spirit walk with the Lord. Sometimes the apostle has to practice relearning subjects they have already been taught with the Holy

Spirit so they can be engaged in the present vision and in the present learning of those around them.
This can be humbling as the apostle has to submit themselves to journeying where the people are, while continuing to live and journey in spiritual dimensions with the Holy Spirit. The enemy loves to make apostles feel like they are all alone and no one understands or can journey with them. When the apostle understands that isolation and loneliness is a part of their kingdom walk, they will avoid challenges with depression and woundedness that comes from having to spend seasons alone. They will also avoid becoming angry, offended, and resentful of people and loved ones who cannot go where they are in God for that season, do not understand it, or become challenged by it.

Speaking of dimensions, apostles experience constant SHIFTS in God. They go from level to level, glory to glory, dimension to dimension continually. Sometimes this can be overwhelming, feel like a roller coaster or race, but most times it is adventurous and fun. Levels are like going to the next street over. Dimensions are like going to the next town – state over. Levels feel like you are elevating in God, while dimensions often feel like you are blasting off like a rocket concerning the things of God. Apostles usually feel as if they are always spiritually treading, towering, and running in the spirit realm, even as they are taking up territory in the natural realm.

The apostle may as well experience a continual pressing upward as they go from levels or dimensions with God. This pressing feels like a constant perseverance, and as the apostle presses, there is a pressing on every side that tends to occur against the apostle.

> ***2Corinthians 3:18*** *But we all, with open face beholding as in a glass the glory of the Lord, are changed into the same image from glory to glory, even as by the Spirit of the Lord.*
>
> ***Phillipians 3:14*** *I press toward the mark for the prize of the high calling of God in Christ Jesus.*
>
> ***1Corinthians 9:24*** *Know ye not that they which run in a race run all, but one receiveth the prize? So run, that ye may obtain.*
>
> ***2Corinthians 4:8*** *We are troubled on every side, yet not distressed; we are perplexed, but not in despair.*

Apostles have the ability to overcome the greatest of adversities. Though they are constantly faced with severe trials, tribulations, and death, they tend to defy every odd. Their lives are in the hands of God, and he uses near death experiences as testimonies of his supernatural power and protection that surrounds the apostle, and how the representation of Jesus is evident upon them.

> ***2Corinthians 4:9-12 The Amplified Bible*** *We are pursued (persecuted and hard driven), but not deserted [to stand alone]; we are struck down to the ground, but never struck out and destroyed; Always carrying about in the body the liability and exposure to the same putting to death that the Lord Jesus suffered, so that the [resurrection] life of Jesus also may be shown forth by and in our bodies.*

> *For we who live are constantly [experiencing] being handed over to death for Jesus' sake, that the [resurrection] life of Jesus also may be evidenced through our flesh which is liable to death. Thus death is actively at work in us, but [it is in order that our] life [may be actively at work] in you.*

Apostles glory in persevering. They enjoy bragging on God and being able to demonstrate the overcoming power of God.

Prayer Impartation: I decree that you are embracing your nature as an apostle. You are embracing all that it entails, and through your embrace, every door to the enemy and wicked people is closed such that they cannot use your character, nature, and calling against you. I decree that as you journey with God, the totality of who you are will be revealed to you. You will know who you are, embrace who you are, live confidently in who you are, and kick devils butts with who you are. Thank you for being an apostle for God's glory. May the perseverance and resurrection power of Jesus encompass your calling and mantle such that you will be a continual testimony of his apostolic grace upon your life. SHIFT!

THE IDENTITY OF AN APOSTLE

Though I shared insight and revelation on the character and nature of the apostle in the previous chapters, it is important to note that there are unique and peculiar attributes about who you are that only God can reveal to you. Though apostles have similar foundations, character traits, and natures, they flow through differenct wells of anointing which makes their identity unique and strategic to the kingdom of God and the world. For example, I flow through the wells of deliverance, warfare and worship, and mantle an apostolic mandate of judging and establishing God's kingdom in people, ministries, communities, and regions. I am called to save, disciple, and raise up kingdom shifters within the younger generation. I am also called to train, equip, and build up the body of Christ in the areas of deliverance, healing, counseling, wellness, fivefold ministry, all manner of prayer, and fine arts. I am also called to scribe teaching manuals such that I leave a legacy of revelation and knowledge in the earth realm that others can glean from. Your well and your mantle may be different from mines even though the nature and characteristics of our apostolic calling may be similar. ***Decreeing God keenly reveals your well and mantle today!***

Identity is the character, nature, truth and essence of who we are. It is the image and prototype of God inside of us. The enemy stole and distorted man's identity in the garden when he tricked Adam and Eve into eating off the tree of knowledge of good and evil.

There lives were open to a new identity of sin and destruction that was not the will of God for their lives (***Genesis 3***). Jesus restored our original identity when he died on the cross and rose to the right hand of the father (***John 2:12, Ephesians 2:5, Colossians 2:9-10, 1Peter 2:9, 1John 3:1-2***). Now that our identity has been restored, we must stand in the truth of our identity and not waver in who we are in God. When the enemy steals or distorts our identity, he steals and alters our calling and destiny in God. When our calling and destiny is stolen or altered, we are not aligned with God. We are unable to effectively operate in who we are in him and who he is in us. The enemy uses this as a legal right to torment us, minimizing our authority and right to tower over him.

Apostles have to know who they are, as the enemy, wicked people, and religious people will come for their identity. They will use the very character and nature of your apostleship as weapons of assault against you. It will also be important for apostles to know who they are so that they can effectively fight the good warfare of faith. Even as apostles study their opponents, they must also study themselves, learn themselves, know their strengths and weaknesses, be clear, certain, and confident about their identity, and who they are in the kingdom of God and to the world.

Because Paul did not walk with Jesus like the other apostles, he had to be sure about his conversion and about his calling as an apostle. Paul also was once a persecutor of Jesus and the disciples. He literally imprisoned and sought to destroy those who preached Jesus. Now that he was converted unto Jesus Christ, and given the unique calling to be an apostle that saved the souls of and preached the gospel to the gentiles, he had to be okay if people did not initially trust him or receive him as an apostle of the faith of Jesus Christ. He still had to walk in his calling and complete the work of the Lord.

> ***Galatians 1:1-2*** *I, Paul, and my companions in faith here, send greetings to the Galatian churches. My authority for writing to you does not come from any popular vote of the people, nor does it come through the appointment of some human higher- up. It comes directly from Jesus the Messiah and God the Father, who raised him from the dead. I'm God- commissioned. So I greet you with the great words, grace and peace!*
>
> ***The Amplified Bible*** *PAUL, AN apostle – [special messenger appointed and commissioned and sent out] not from [any body of] men nor by or through any man, but by and through Jesus Christ (the Messiah) and God the Father, Who raised Him from among the dead – And all the brethren who are with me, to the churches of Galatia: Grace and spiritual blessing be to you and [soul] peace from God the Father and our Lord Jesus Christ (the Messiah),*

As Apostle Paul released his message to the church, he spoke these words about his identity:

Verse 10-20 The Amplified Bible *Now am I trying to win the favor of men, or of God? Do I seek to please men? If I were still seeking popularity with men, I should not be a bond servant of Christ (the Messiah). For I want you to know, brethren, that the Gospel which was proclaimed and made known by me is not man's gospel [a human invention, according to or patterned after any human standard]. For indeed I did not receive it from man, nor was I taught it, but* *[it came to me] through a [direct] revelation [given] by Jesus Christ (the Messiah).*

You have heard of my earlier career and former manner of life in the Jewish religion (Judaism), how I persecuted and abused the church of God furiously and extensively, and [with fanatical zeal did my best] to make havoc of it and destroy it. And [you have heard how] I outstripped many of the men of my own generation among the people of my race in [my advancement in study and observance of the laws of] Judaism, so extremely enthusiastic and zealous I was for the traditions of my ancestors.

But when He, Who had chosen and set me apart [even] before I was born and had called me by His grace (His undeserved favor and blessing), saw fit and was pleased. To reveal (unveil, disclose) His Son within me so that I might proclaim Him among the Gentiles (the non-Jewish world) as the glad tidings (Gospel), immediately I did not confer with flesh and blood [did not consult or counsel with any frail human being or communicate with anyone].

Nor did I [even] go up to Jerusalem to those who were apostles (special messengers of Christ) before I was, but I went away and retired into Arabia, and afterward I came back again to Damascus. Then three years later, I did go up to Jerusalem to become [personally] acquainted with Cephas (Peter), and remained with him for fifteen days. But I did not see any of the other apostles (the special messengers of Christ) except James the brother of our Lord. Now [note carefully what I am telling you, for it is the truth], I write this as if I were standing before the bar of God; I do not lie.

Like Apostle, Paul, I too was initially chosen and sent by Jesus Christ. It was not until years later that I was confirmed by man, established by man, and further released by man into my calling and destiny. Even as I am constantly confirmed by my overseer, because of the wounds of my past, I had a couple years where I was waiting for her to tell me I was a farce and my entire walk and identity was a figment of my imagination.

Many of you have the same testimony and like me, the journey has not be easy, but you have been obedient. Because I was not clear in my identity, I did not have the boldness of Apostle Paul concerning my calling. I was not able to articulate it, and often times my very identity, calling, visions, and works God granted to my hands, were used to persecute and hinder me in the ministry endeavors of the Lord. I always completed God's work whether accepted by man or not. But I admit that I desired man's approval, favor, and validation. I wanted them to initially believe and empower what God was doing through me, and not wait for the signs, wonders, and successes, to approve me. And even then, others would take credit for works I completed. I was challenged by this, but accepted that God was pleased with me, and that people knew the truth even if they did not acknowledge it.

> **Galatians 1:10** *For do I now persuade men, or God? or do I seek to please men? for if I yet pleased men, I should not be the servant of Christ.*

Apostle Paul said *"**do I now persuade men or God?**"* Because the apostolic has not been readily received in the body of Christ, it is easy to get into trying to persuade people of who you are. Thankfully I never yielded to persuading people I was an apostle. I generally rejected it and felt ashamed and inferior of my calling. This is not good either as doing this steals your authority and ability to sufficiently conquer over demonic forces. They respond to authority and if you reject it then you cannot walk in the truth of your victory and authority through God.

When persuading, we are striving to convince, coax, brainwash, impress, and manipulate people into receiving who we are. Their receptivity of us is not genuine as it is rooted in the insecurity of who we are convincing them we are, rather than the true identity of who we are. We therefore, have to keep performing so that they can be further persuaded of our identities and we become puppets of their opinions of us as opposed to realities of the identification of Jesus Christ. Apostle Paul refused to succumb to this type of behavior.

Apostle Paul was even given revelation by God that he was called at birth.

> **Galatians 1:15** *But when it pleased God, who separated me from my mother's womb, and called me by his grace, To reveal his Son in me, that I might preach him among the heathen; immediately I conferred not with flesh and blood.*

Many apostles can look back over their lives and realize that the calling of God has always been upon them – that the commission of Jesus Christ has always been their portion. At this time in his journey, Apostle Paul did not need man to validate this truth for him. He was being validated as he was in Holy Spirit school with the Lord. The greatest key we can take from Apostle Paul's story is that even though he once persecuted saints, because he operated in confidence concerning his identity, those who knew his past still embraced him and as he stated in *Verse 23*, *"glorified the God in him."* They honored him.

When we understand our identity and boldly walk in it, though there will be those that will persecute us, there will also be those who will honor us. Honor of this magnitude and through a pure well confirms and validates the calling upon our lives. And such honor will come through those we did not expect it to. They will see clearly who we are and will glorify the God in us.

At the leading of the Lord, Apostle Paul eventually visited the elite apostles. They too honored and recognized that the gospel he was preaching was the same they were teaching to the Jews. They confirmed him through the giving of the right hand of fellowship, which was a way of making covenant with him as an apostle of Jesus Christ. They however, could not really add anything else to what Jesus himself had already taught and revealed to Apostle Paul through his life journey in Holy Spirit school.

> ***Galatians 2:2-10 New Living Translation*** *I went there because God revealed to me that I should go. While I was there I met privately with those considered to be leaders of the church and shared with them the message I had been preaching to the Gentiles. I wanted to make sure that we were in agreement, for fear that all my efforts had been wasted and I was running the race for nothing. And they supported me and did not even demand that my companion Titus be circumcised, though he was a Gentile. Even that question came up only because of some so-called Christians there – false*

ones, really — who were secretly brought in. They sneaked in to spy on us and take away the freedom we have in Christ Jesus. They wanted to enslave us and force us to follow their Jewish regulations. But we refused to give in to them for a single moment. We wanted to preserve the truth of the gospel message for you.

And the leaders of the church had nothing to add to what I was preaching. (By the way, their reputation as great leaders made no difference to me, for God has no favorites). Instead, they saw that God had given me the responsibility of preaching the gospel to the Gentiles, just as he had given Peter the responsibility of preaching to the Jews. For the same God who worked through Peter as the apostle to the Jews also worked through me as the apostle to the Gentiles.

In fact, James, Peter,[c] and John, who were known as pillars of the church, recognized the gift God had given me, and they accepted Barnabas and me as their co-workers. They encouraged us to keep preaching to the Gentiles, while they continued their work with the Jews. Their only suggestion was that we keep on helping the poor, which I have always been eager to do.

When Apostle Paul went to connect with the elite apostles, he was not worried about whether he was called to be an apostle. He was confident in his calling and did not need or desire their approval. Apostle Paul's main concern was whether he was teaching sound and correct doctrine that identified and glorified Jesus. When we are confident in our identity, this is where our focus will be.

Even as false christians came to incite question regarding Apostle Paul by suggesting Titus be circumcised in the likeness of the Jewish faith, Apostle Paul did not waver in the freedom and liberty he had acquired in his identity and calling with Jesus Christ. The apostles also respected his liberty, and did not use the legalism of circumcision as a catalyst for him proving his identity. Apostle Paul actually stated that *"we wanted to preserve the truth of the gospel message for you."* We do not allow others to alter our identity and experience in Holy Spirit life school with the Lord, we are preserving the truth of the gospel message that has been instilled in us. It remains pure and undefiled by religion and manmade rules, regulations, twisted doctrines, and perversions.

The elite apostles also did not seek to add to the knowledge and revelation that Apostle Paul had already obtained from Jesus through Holy Spirit life school. True leaders who respect the calling and life of an apostle, will not seek to add to what Jesus has and is doing in that apostle. They will only confirm and further encourage them in what God is doing. They will empower you in your identity and calling as an apostle, and partner with you to ensure that God's work in and through you is established in the earth. They will also receive those who complete the work of the kingdom with you and leave you in Jesus's hands to further be trained, equipped, empowered, and released into the work of the kingdom.

Apostle Paul did not show himself to be inferior to the apostles as he knew that his calling had just as must value as their's did. He was liberated from the approval of man through his journey with Jesus Christ, and he was not going to allow insecurities to restrict and bind him in religion, and the entanglements of the persuasions of man. This is so vital as often we let people negate our personal equipping with Jesus Christ as not sufficient to going to seminary, or having someone initially identify us as an apostle. The enemy is quick to use this to coward us or make us hesitant in operating in our calling. But we must recognize that Holy Spirit life school actually delivered us from religion and the clamps of man. God always tells me that because I have journeyed in Holy Spirit life school with him, no one will ever be able to take credit for what he has and will do through me. I have learned to embraced this as a blessing as even though I would love more supports, and connections, and affiliates pouring into me, I never want to feel like I owe anyone or that I am owned by anyone. My identity and calling belongs to God, and only he can take credit for who I am and who I will become.

> ***Galatians 3:1-6*** *Oh, foolish Galatians! Who has cast an evil spell on you? For the meaning of Jesus Christ's death was made as clear to you as if you had seen a picture of his death on the cross. Let me ask you this one question: Did you receive the Holy Spirit by obeying the law of Moses? Of course not! You received the Spirit because you believed the message you heard about Christ.*
>
> *How foolish can you be? After starting your Christian lives in the Spirit, why are you now trying to become perfect by your own human effort? Have you experienced so much for nothing? Surely it was not in vain, was it? Have you experienced so much for nothing? Surely it was not in vain, was it? I ask you*

again, does God give you the Holy Spirit and work miracles among you because you obey the law? Of course not! It is because you believe the message you heard about Christ.

APOSTLE! It is bewitchment to return to the religious systems and the dictatorship of man. Jesus has delivered you, called you, trained you, equipped you, validated you, and released you. He works in, through, and with you as you complete the work of the kingdom. People can further confirm and release who you are, but they can never take the place of Holy Spirit in your life. Know your identity so you can identify those who seek to rob you of your truth in God, and all he has personally put in you even when you were in your mother's womb. **YOU ARE JESUS' APOSTLE AND THERE IS NOTHING THE DEVIL AND PEOPLE CAN DO ABOUT IT! SHIFT INTO BEING AND COMPLETELY ACCEPTING YOU! SHIFT!**

Apostolic Exploration:

1. Who are you as an apostle in God? What are the wells of anointing you operate through? What is your calling?
2. Journal your story of Jesus and the Holy Spirit inducting you into apostleship.
3. What are the truths concerning your identity as a person? As an apostle?
4. What areas in your identity need healing? Seek God concerning these areas and ask him for a plan to heal and build your confidence in your identity.
5. Explore and journal your past hurts with being rejected and devalued in your apostolic experience.

What reasons do you need the validation of man? Seek God for healing in these areas.
6. Study the life of Apostle Paul. Journal what you learned about his story and how it relates to your life.
7. Write a identity decree about who you are as an apostle. Include the following topics:
    a. Your call as an apostle
    b. Your call to the church
    c. Your call to people
    d. Your call to your region & spheres of influence
    e. Your call to the nations (if applicable)
    f. Your call to the world (if applicable)
    g. The purpose of your call to each area
    h. The generational heritage you are to leave in the earth
8. Decree out identity decree every week until it becomes your truth.

THE APOSTOLIC MANTLE

When many refer to their spiritual mantle, they speak of and envision it as a cloak, cape, or even a coat. Though this may not be the case for every apostle, spiritually I see apostles blanketed in their mantles as if it was a literally armor embodiment. It feels like and looks like the entire body has been engulfed in the mantle, and at times it looks more like a suite of armor, while other times it is a huge covering of some sort. The mantle seems to have compartments that enable the apostle to become or do what Jesus is requiring at the time. The mantle feels very weighty at times, and looks very heavy. Yet, there seems to be a supernatural strength upon the apostle to sufficiently carry the mantle.

> ***Psalms 18:32*** *It is God that girdeth (mantle) me with strength, and maketh my way perfect.*

Girdeth is âzar; in the Hebrew and means:

1. to belt: — bind (compass) about, gird (up, with).
2. bind about, compass about, encompass, equip, clothe
3. gird on (metaphorical of strength)
    a. (Qal) to gird
    b. (Niphal) be girded
    c. (Piel) hold close, clasp
    d. (Hiphpael) gird oneself (for war)
    e.

Strength is *haiyl* in the Hebrew and means:

1. a force, whether of men, means or other resources
2. an army, wealth, virtue, valor, strength
3. able, activity, band of men (soldiers), company, (great) forces
4. goods, host, might, power, riches, strong, substance, train
5. valiant (- ly), valour, virtuous (- ly), war, worthy (-ily), efficiency, ability

When we are girded in our mantle, it is the truth of God that is upon us. This truth yields eternal life, therefore, the mantle is ALIVE and never dies. This is the reason the mantle can be passed down from generation to generation and transferred to successors. THE MANTLE IS ETERNALLY ALIVE!

Through the girding truth of God, the mantle encompasses us with the character, nature, power, and presence of God. Because the mantle is bonded – belted – surrounded about us, the mantle itself is a very intimate apparel. It is personal and possesses intricate and intimate parts of who we are in God and who God is within us as his apostles. Because the mantle encompasses about the apostle, it has an aroma, presentation, and stature. It therefore, possesses anointing oils and governmental authorities that distinguishes the apostle's aura and rank in the spirit realm and in the earth.

Mantles equip the apostle spiritually and naturally to operate in and govern the calling that is upon their life. We do not have to succumb to our human strength, or feel pressured or inadequate in our duties. Naturally, it may not appear that we can carry or complete the call that is upon our lives, but God has perfected us. We in essence, can cast these perceptions down as dung because the mantle gives us supernatural powers and abilities to defy every obstacle.

> *Verse 32 New Living Translation God arms me with strength, and he makes my way perfect.*

> *Verse 32 The Message Bible Is there any god like God? Are we not at bedrock? Is not this the God who armed me, then aimed me in the right direction?*

The mantle is an armor, which for the apostle makes sense, as the mantle and even our literal beings feel like a strategic weapon at times. God engulfs the apostle inside the mantle and arms him or her as a living weapon – equipped for the task at hand.

> *Jeremiah 51:20 Thou art my battle axe (smiter) and weapons of war: for with thee will I break in pieces the nations, and with thee will I destroy kingdoms;*

The mantle upon the apostle is violent. This is another reason for the processing, death, and resurrection of the apostle. We must be equipped to face danger fiercely, and though meek and humble, we must be clear that our lives are an annihilation to every enemy of Jesus.

> *Matthew 11:12 And from the days of John the Baptist until now the kingdom of heaven suffereth violence, and the violent take it by force.*

> ***New Living Translation*** *And from the time John the Baptist began preaching until now, the Kingdom of Heaven has been forcefully advancing, and violent people are attacking it.*

Part of the apostle's mandate is to preach that the kingdom of God is at hand (***Matthew 10:7***). Therefore, the apostle should know that it is his or her lifestyle duty to take the kingdom by force.

Violent is *biastes* in Greek and means an *"energetic strong forcer."*

Dictionary.com defines *violent* as:

1. acting with or characterized by uncontrolled, strong, rough force
2. someone causes injurious or destructive force
3. intense in force, effect, etc.; severe; extreme
4. roughly or immoderately vehement or ardent
5. furious in impetuosity (rash or impulsive action), energy, etc.
6. something that distorts a meaning or fact

As we consider this definition, we can discern that a violent person is not waiting on a fight, but they are looking, expecting, and even anxious to fight; some people will even provoke a fight to get the battle started.

A violent person is jealous for the things they want to possess. They do not want anyone else with it; they do not trust anyone with it. They take drastic measures to annihilate any and all competition.

A violent person is expecting to assert control over every situation; they are expecting to intimidate, defend, and even to conquer a matter.

A violent person feels justified in his or her actions. Even if it is not a correct or realistic justification, a violent person believes they

- have a right to behave the way they do
- have a right to take what they want
- and have a right to control and unleash wrath on a person or situation.

A violent person is not waiting to be given something. They live offensively in overthrowing and overpowering whatever it is they desire, need, or feel should be theirs.

Most often a violent person does not take responsibility for their actions. They often blame their actions on the victim, their circumstances, their past, or their heritage. And if they do accept responsibility, there is generally an ulterior motive behind it. Their apology is just another strategy to manipulate, control, and further subdue the victim under their authority.

A violent person does not just control people and the atmosphere when they are around. They have unleashed so much terror, violence, and control that people obey them even when they are not around. The atmospheres and cultures to which they have asserted authority, remains subdued even when they are not physically there. Sometimes long after they are gone, a person or atmosphere is still subdued by the stronghold of their actions. Their actions can have generational impact, not just on their family lineage, but on the victim's family lineage.

A violent person has identified and knows how to use their weapons of choice. Though they can be explosive, and improvise on impulse, they know the weapons of their warfare, whether it be their hands, a knife, a gun, a machete, a hammer, poison, a sword, torture. They know what weapons they work best with, and even have an arsenal of weaponry, and plethora of choices on hand the more they mature as a violent offender.

A violent person does not mind slinging threats. They make sure you know what they are capable of. They are clear in their abilities and letting it be known that they will have their way by any means necessary.

A violent person will sacrifice their life for what they are passionate about. They are willing to render their life and their freedom for it. They are not willing to allow the enemy or even the law the satisfaction of taking them out. They will kill their enemy then themselves before they allow their pursuer to assert any justice or authority over their lives.

A violent person is extremely dangerous because you never know what they are thinking or feeling, and you never know when they are going to fly off the handle, or pop their lid. They are unpredictable, meek one minute and explosive the next; they are moody, and even if you wait to see what mood their in before you engage them, they can shift on you at any time.

It is like walking on egg shells around a violent person as you are not trying to set them off and you are not sure what will set them off. Even though they have weapons, they are the weapon. They are a ticking time bomb ready to explode at any moment.

As we consider the violent mantle, it is important to note that the calling and mantle upon the apostle is that of warfare.

> **2Corinthians 10:3-4** *For though we walk in the flesh, we do not war after the flesh: (For the weapons of our warfare are not carnal, but mighty through God to the pulling down of strong holds).*

<u>*Warfare* is *strateia* in the Greek and means:</u>

1. military service, i.e. (figuratively) the apostolic career (as one of hardship and danger): — warfare
2. an expedition, campaign, military service, warfare
3. metaph. Paul likens his contest with the difficulties that oppose him in the discharge of his apostolic duties, as warfare

Apostle Paul is contending that it is the essence of his apostolic calling to be opposed and to fight as one living a career in a military service.

Most saints equate warfare as:

- Being out of the will of God or in sin
- Not having enough faith or maturity concerning the things of God
- Being in demonic oppression or bondage
- An indicator that we are not successful or we are failing in our destiny or ministry

- Or we do not adequately discern when warfare is not about our destiny and calling such that we are not aware of open doors in our lives and ministries

Apostles must count these perceptions as dung. **APOSTLE!** Warfare is a part of your mantle and calling. There are no wimpy apostles, as apostles are mantled to be violent. There is not one apostle that avoids warfare. If someone is contending they are an apostle, and do not engage in warfare or contend they do not have warfare, they are not an apostle. The mantle is violent therefore, your very presentation will provoke fights with demons, enemies of Jesus Christ, and wickedness. If knowing that your life is a weapon of destruction is not enough, meditate on these truths of your power and authority over ever enemy as a believer and an apostle.

> *Luke 10:19 Behold, I give you the authority to trample on serpents and scorpions, and over all the power of the enemy, and nothing shall by any means hurt you.*
>
> *Psalms 2:8 Ask of me, and I shall give thee the heathen for thine inheritance, and the uttermost parts of the earth for thy possession.*
>
> *Psalms 144:2 My goodness, and my fortress; my high tower, and my deliverer; my shield, and he in whom I trust; who subdueth my people under me.*
>
> *Deuteronomy 33:29 New American Standard Bible Blessed are you, O Israel; Who is like you, a people saved by the LORD, Who is the shield of your help And the*

sword of your majesty! So your enemies will cringe before you, And you will tread upon their high places.

Take a moment apostle and consider your mantle and your life. Are you violent enough for the spheres and people God has granted to your hands?

Apostle, are you truly offensive in taking the kingdom by force?

- Are you predictable where the devil and people are not even swayed by what you bring to this world?
- When you minister, is the kingdom of God invading your midst, being established, transforming lives, atmospheres, and regions?
- As you search yourself, ask God to empower you all the more as a violent apostle.
- Ask God to give you insight and foresight concerning your apostolic mantle and how to be an even greater destructive force for his glory.

The Mantle Has Blueprints

The mantle comes with its own blueprint of instructions and standards for its upkeep, protection and fortification, and the sustaining of its purity. The mantle comes with vision, clear life plans, accountability, and personal responsibility. The mantle will tell you what you can and cannot do, what you can and cannot be involved in, what you can and cannot be surrounded by, and what you can and cannot consume. The mantle will set you a part and consecrate you. And the mantle will depart from you if you do not take care of it, value it, and make it a priority of your life to follow its blueprint and maintain its vision.

> ***Judges 13:2-5*** *And there was a certain man of Zorah, of the family of the Danites, whose name was Manoah; and his wife was barren, and bare not. And the angel of the Lord appeared unto the woman, and said unto her, Behold now, thou art barren, and bearest not: but thou shalt conceive, and bear a son. Now therefore beware, I pray thee, and drink not wine nor strong drink, and eat not any unclean thing: For, lo, thou shalt conceive, and bear a son; and no razor shall come on his head: for the child shall be a Nazarite unto God from the womb: and he shall begin to deliver Israel out of the hand of the Philistines.*

> ***Judges 16:19*** *And she made him sleep upon her knees; and she called for a man, and she caused him to shave off the seven locks of his head; and she began to afflict him, and his strength went from him.*

Mantles Establish Nations & Advance God's Kingdom

As violent apostles called and positioned to take the world by force, we must know that God has mantled us to establish his will into nations and to advance his kingdom.

> ***Psalms 18:39*** *For thou hast girded me with strength unto the battle: thou hast subdued under me those that rose up against me.*

Mantles Yield God Glory

> ***Isaiah 45:5-6 The Amplified Bible*** *I am the Lord, and there is no one else; there is no God besides Me. I will gird and arm you, though you have not known Me, That men may know from the east and the rising of the sun and from the west and the setting of the sun that there is no God besides Me. I am the Lord, and no one else [is He].*

> ***New English Translation*** *I am the Lord, I have no peer, there is no God but me. I arm you for battle, even though you do not recognize me. I do this so people will recognize from east to west that there is no God but me; I am the Lord, I have no peer.*

> ***2Kings 2:14*** *And he took the mantle of Elijah that fell from him, and smote the waters, and said, Where is the LORD God of Elijah? and when he also had smitten the waters, they parted hither and thither: and Elisha went over.*

Mantles Open Supernatural Pathways

> ***2Kings 2:8*** *Elijah took his mantle and folded it together and struck the waters, and they were divided here and there, so that the two of them crossed over on dry ground.*

We also see from this passage that mantles create pathways for us to shift on solid and safe ground.

The Mantle Is Ordained & Will Find You

The mantle is ordained by God and will find you. When you are doing life just like any other day, working, taking care of family, going to school and etc. the mantle will hurl itself upon you and change your entire life. It will be cast and thrown upon you with such force and such life altering thrust that it will cause you to drop all that you know and have known for the sake of following it. The mantle will cause you to forsake all and be shifted into the beginning of what seems like an utterly brand new life.

> ***1Kings 19:19-21*** *So he departed thence, and found Elisha the son of Shaphat, who was plowing with twelve yoke of oxen before him, and he with the twelfth: and Elijah passed by him, and cast his mantle upon him. And he left the oxen, and ran after Elijah, and said, Let me, I pray thee, kiss my father and my mother, and then I will follow thee. And he said unto him, Go back again: for what have I done to thee? And he returned back from him, and took a yoke of oxen, and slew them, and boiled their flesh with the instruments of the oxen, and gave unto the people, and they did eat. Then he arose, and went after Elijah, and ministered unto him.*

The Mantle Protects You

The mantle comforts, covers and protects you, even from the Lord at times. It serves as an armor of authority for you in the times of storms and uncertainty. It graces you with mercy when you need

God's still small voice. It comforts you when you fear the unknown.

> **1Kings 19:13** *When Elijah heard it, he wrapped his face in his mantle and went out and stood in the entrance of the cave And behold, a voice came to him and said, "What are you doing here, Elijah?"*

Mantles Can Be Prostituted

You can misuse and prostitute your mantle; you can infect others with a defiled mantle. You can take what is meant to be for God - given as a pure gift from God - and offer it up as a sacrifice to idol gods, even offering up the generations through the misuse of your mantle.

> **Ezekiel 16:15-21** *But thou didst trust in thine own beauty, and playedst the harlot because of thy renown, and pouredst out thy fornications on every one that passed by; his it was. And of thy garments thou didst take, and deckedst thy high places with divers colours, and playedst the harlot thereupon: the like things shall not come, neither shall it be so.*
>
> *Thou hast also taken thy fair jewels (gifts) of my gold and of my silver (purified gifts), which I had given thee, and madest to thyself images of men, and didst commit whoredom with them, And tookest thy broidered garments, and coveredst them (protected and mantled the idol): and thou hast set mine oil and mine incense before them. My meat also which I gave thee, fine flour, and oil, and honey, wherewith I fed thee, thou hast even set it before them for a sweet savour (meaning you desired to please the idol with your mantle and the*

things that belonged to God): and thus it was, saith the Lord God.

Moreover thou hast taken thy sons and thy daughters, whom thou hast borne unto me, and these hast thou sacrificed unto them to be devoured. Is this of thy whoredoms a small matter, That thou hast slain my children and delivered them to cause them to pass through the fire for them? (The generations were sacrificed and destroyed through the misuse of the mantle).

- You can prostitute your mantle by using it for anything other than what it was designed for such that the mantle itself becomes an idol.

Ezekiel 16:16 New Living Translation You used the lovely things I gave you to make shrines for idols, where you played the prostitute. Unbelievable! How could such a thing ever happen?

- You can offer your mantle up as a sacrifice unto idols and become comfortable with going to hell.

Isaiah 57:7-9 Upon a lofty and high mountain hast thou set (made) thy bed (became comfortable in sleeping in idolatry): even thither wentest thou up to offer sacrifice (you left destiny for the high place). Behind the doors also and the posts (the secret place-the secret sins) hast thou set up thy remembrance: for thou hast discovered thyself to another than me, and art gone up (become your own God and a worker of the devil); thou hast enlarged thy bed (got a whole lot of people sharing your mantle, the personal distinguishing things regarding who you are), and made thee a covenant with them (a vowing relationship); thou lovedst their bed where thou sawest it. And thou wentest to the king with ointment, and didst increase thy perfumes (demonic kings are receiving the oil from your mantle), and didst send thy messengers far off, and didst debase thyself even unto hell.

You Can Betray Jesus With Your Mantle

Apostle Judas walked with Jesus, fellowshipped with Jesus, feasted with Jesus, sat at the feet of Jesus, was trained and equipped by Jesus, ministered with and for Jesus, yet he sacrificed his position, relationship, calling, and destiny for money. He used his mantle to identify and deliver Jesus into the hands of his enemies (***Mark 14***). He violated his relationship with Jesus and the mantle that was upon is life by pursuing a path that was not honoring or submitted to God, and that would persecute and kill Jesus' name rather than glorify it.

> ***Acts 1:24-25*** *And they prayed, and said, Thou, Lord, which knowest the hearts of all men, shew whether of these two thou hast chosen, That he may take part of this ministry and apostleship, from which Judas by transgression fell, that he might go to his own place.*
>
> ***The Message Bible*** *Then they prayed, "You, O God, know every one of us inside and out. Make plain which of these two men you choose to take the place in this ministry and leadership that Judas threw away in order to go his own way."*

The Consequences Of Disobedience Regarding The Mantle

When you run from an assignment, you are in disobedience, and are betraying the mantle that is upon your life. You are also rejecting your identity and calling as the mantle is a part of you. There are times where the mantle may not chase after you. Then there are instances where grace abounds and the mantle will find you, and close in all around you until you have no choice but to say yes. You must say yes to the mantle so that God's will can be done in the earth through you. Jonah was placed into the belly of a whale because he dropped his mantle and ran. When you run from the mantle and God's grace is activated, the mantle will trap you in the midst of an unusual supernatural environment or circumstance such that you will have to inwardly digest, process, and surrender to the mantle.

> *Jonah 1:1-3* *Now the word of the Lord came unto Jonah the son of Amittai, saying, Arise, go to Nineveh, that great city, and cry against it; for their wickedness is come up before me. But Jonah rose up to flee unto Tarshish from the presence of the Lord, and went down to Joppa; and he found a ship going to Tarshish: so he paid the fare thereof, and went down into it, to go with them unto Tarshish from the presence of the Lord.*

> *Jonah 1:17* *Now the Lord had prepared a great fish to swallow up Jonah. And Jonah was in the belly of the fish three days and three nights.*

The Mantle Can Be Stripped

Since the mantle is a girding, it only sticks to us if we have the right stuff in us to bind it to us. It therefore, can become loose. It can come off, for God does not take gifts for they are without repentance (**Romans 11:29**), but he does strip us of our mantles.

> **1Corinthians 9:26** *But I keep under my body, and bring it into subjection: lest that by any means, when I have preached to others, I myself should be a castaway.*

Castaway means *"unapproved, not approved, rejected, worthless, reprobate, unfit, not standing the test."*

Saul was a castaway. In *1Samuel 15*, God rejected Saul because of his disobedience. God stripped his mantle, his position, and his kingdom. And though he was king for multiple years after being stripped, the fruit, favor, and approval of God did not follow him. It however, followed David who God mantled to be king in his stead.

Tearing Of The Mantle

- Sometimes, man will seek to strip you of your mantle - tear, abuse, or destroy the mantle of your identity and calling, and the very mantle will become a prophetic sign of their own judgment and shame.

> **1Samuel 15:27-28** *And as Samuel turned about to go away, he laid hold upon the skirt of his mantle, and it rent. And Samuel said unto him, The Lord hath rent the*

> kingdom of Israel from thee this day, and hath given it to a neighbour of thine, that is better than thou.

- Sometimes you will have to tear the mantle and strip yourself in submission and reverence to God.

> ***Ezra 9:3*** *When I heard about this matter, I tore my garment and my robe, and pulled some of the hair from my head and my beard, and sat down appalled.*

> ***Job 1:20*** *Then Job arose and tore his robe and shaved his head, and he fell to the ground and worshiped.*

The Mantle Has Haters

People will hate you because of your mantle. Joseph brothers put him in a pit, then sold him into slavery because of his mantle.

> ***Genesis 37:3-4*** *Now Israel loved Joseph more than all his children, because he was the son of his old age: and he made him a coat of many colours. And when his brethren saw that their father loved him more than all his brethren, they hated him, and could not speak peaceably unto him.*

The Mantle Will Be Tested

The mantle will be tested, tempted, and tried. God told Abraham that he would have descendants as numerous as the stars in the sky. He was to be the father of many nations, and in the midst of that great word, God required him to sacrifice his son – the mantle of the promise upon his life. He was obedient to the direction of the Lord even though it seemed to be contrary to the word he was given about his descendants. He trusted the Lord, presented Issac before him, and as he raised his hand to slay Issac, the Lord stayed his hand.   The the Lord provided a ram in the bush and spared Issac's life. The mantle will be tested as God wants to know do we love the mantle more than him. We are to put our trust in the Lord and not in the mantle. God will preserve the mantle and cause it to flourish upon us.

> *Genesis 26:4 And I will make thy seed to multiply as the stars of heaven, and will give unto thy seed all these countries; and in thy seed shall all the nations of the earth be blessed;*

> *Genesis 22:1-2 And it came to pass after these things, that God did tempt Abraham, and said unto him, Abraham: and he said, Behold, here I am. And he said, Take now thy son, thine only son Isaac, whom thou lovest, and get thee into the land of Moriah; and offer him there for a burnt offering upon one of the mountains which I will tell thee of.*

The Devil Will Come For The Mantle

The devil will send hardship so you will unnecessarily strip yourself of your mantle as he wants to defile and kill your destiny. We see this when Amnon rapes his half sister Tamar and she strips herself of her mantle.

> *2Samuel 13:18-19 And she had a garment of divers colours upon her: for with such robes were the king's daughters that were virgins apparelled. Then his servant*

brought her out, and bolted the door after her. And Tamar put ashes on her head, and rent her garment of divers colours that was on her, and laid her hand on her head, and went on crying.

Because the enemy is after our mantles, apostles must be violent mantle carriers. We must take them up, enmesh in covenant with them, remain eternally enveloped in them; and know that they make us literal weapons against the enemy, and kingdom establishers for God's glory.

Apostolic Mantle Prayer: Decreeing you have gained increased insight and revelation concerning your apostolic calling and personal mantle. Decreeing you have SHIFTED into the fullness of its engulfment upon your life, while being armored with new limitless authority, ability, power, and resource to beat devils down and take God's kingdom by force. **SHIFT!**

UNHEALTHY VERSUS HEALED APOSTLE
Taquetta Baker's Journey As A Wounded But Determined Apostle

I want to sincerely note that anything I share about my apostolic journey is not to tear down any person or ministry, as I am truly grateful and blessed for all the opportunities and hands on training I have received. In many ways, that in and of itself, helped to identify and develop me as an apostle. The opportunities and hands on training also enabled me to learn the tools, keys, and insight that I am now utilizing and releasing to empower other upcoming apostles and fivefold ministry offices.

As an upcoming apostle, I walked as a wounded leader determined to be healthy. I did not have revelation that I was an apostle and identification from those around me that the apostolic calling was upon my life. I did not have empowerment in my identity, mentoring, equipping or training as an apostle. At the time, I did not have the revelation that I wrote about in this book regarding being at peace with Jesus identifying me and the Holy Spirit mentoring, training and equipping me as an apostle. I did receive ministry training at times and prophetic training within my local church. But much of what I learned as an apostle was hands on. Though I knew the works I was completing were apostolic in nature, I did not know they were demonstrating that I was an apostle. I assumed I was able to pioneer, trail blaze, plant, plow, produce, and have continual visions for works that needed to be completed due to operating through the apostolic grace that was upon the church. I also gleaned from various apostolic ministries within the body of Christ, to which I assumed strengthened the grace upon me, and caused me to operate with such apostolic force. I did not realize at the time that all my life I was pioneering, trail blazing, leading the pack, and mentoring others. I was just doing whatever God would grant me to do. And with that, I had my leaders' permissive will, but I did not have their support. They gave me permission to do what God granted to my hands, but did not support, empower, or guide me in it. There is a huge difference between permission and support.

Dictionary.com defines *permission:*
1. authorization granted to do something; formal consent
2. to allow to do something
3. to allow to be done or occur
4. to tolerate; agree to
5. to afford opportunity for, or possibility, or admit of

Permission can appear as if it is support and release, but really it is just consent and allowance to do something. Someone can allow you to do a work and not necessarily uphold that work, agree with that work, engage in that work, understand who you are in God, identify your calling, mentor you in that work, equip or release you in your calling even though they permit you to complete that assignment.

Dictionary.com defines *support* as:
1. to bear or hold up (a load, mass, structure, part, etc.); serve as a foundation for
2. to sustain or withstand (weight, pressure, strain,

etc.) without giving way; serve as a prop for
3. to undergo or endure, especially with patience or submission; tolerate
4. to sustain (a person, the mind, spirits, courage, etc.) under trial or affliction
5. to maintain (a person, family, establishment, institution, etc.) by supplying with things necessary to existence; provide for
6. to uphold (a person, cause, policy, etc.) by aid, countenance, one's vote, etc.; back; second
7. to maintain or advocate (a theory, principle, etc.)
8. to corroborate (a statement, opinion, etc.)
9. to act with or second (a lead performer); assist in performance

Support means you are actually engaged in the work. You are
- Interested in how it is processing and progressing
- Holding the vision up in prayer, while interceding for the vision to come to pass
- Providing suggestions, guidance, mentoring, and insight as God leads
- Advocating for the work
- Undergirding and bearing it up emotionally, financially, spiritually, etc.
- Assisting where necessary and offering assistance to demonstrate your support

Though I had permission, I received no support from leadership in the works I was pioneering, trail blazing, etc. I was the one giving my leaders the vision for the work, then implementing them as the Holy Spirit led. Because I was in a church that had SHIFTED from being a part of the Pentecostal Assemblies of the World to fivefold apostolic ministry, they too were learning, pioneering, and trail blazing as they embarked upon a new spiritual territory. My leaders loved the Lord and sacrificed their lives for the work of the kingdom. They had a drive and focus to see the kingdom of God advance. I do not believe it was their heart to only grant me permission. They too were receiving hands on training regarding the apostolic, so we both were learning as we went along with Jesus. With hands on learning it is easy to return to the familiar. It is very easy to fumble your way through when you do not have clear vision, have an old vision that is combating your new vision, or do not have true vision of the new that is before you. This new territory was unfamiliar and there was no definitive earthly model. Though the focus of the church was to be apostolic, there was also the reverting of operating in the old pastoral Pentecostal paradigm. There is not much undergirding and equipping in such a paradigm. You are granted permission, then thrown into the deep to do the work of the Lord. There is not much team in that paradigm. Sometimes the religious spirits, doctrines, mindsets, and residue of that paradigm will combat that which is new and challenge those who are trail blazing for change and complete liberation in the works of God. That is what happened to me. And because I had no Pentecostal or apostolic foundation, God had to teach me how to maneuver through the challenges I was experiencing. He also had to teach me how not to be so "gung ho," aka eager, that I put myself in harms way of contention. This also causes wounds – unnecessary ones. I learned this the hard way, as I was not indoctrinated. So the God I was learning about and life I living was one of freedom, and I wanted everyone to have what I had and to have what Jesus was showing me we could all have. This is where my fervor and the apostolic identity that was within me would cause me to push pass where most were ready to go. I had to learn to pace myself and to push in the spirit realm through warfare and intercession, while granting grace and compassion naturally to those who needed a processing into where God was taking us as a body of saints.

Sidebar Comment: I learned over time that whether we know it or not, we are our own apostolic model. We can glean from others, but we are our own model. The *Acts 2* church was its own model. We will gain revelation and tools from their biblical foundation of the apostolic, but we will still be our own model. This is the reason it is important to receive clear vision and continual direction from Jesus. It is also important to totally let go of anything you think you know - old doctrines and religious paradigms, and to trust God to teach you and guide you with what you do not know. You may glean from this book, but you have to take what you learn and apply it to the apostolic model inside of you as Jesus leads.

Okay back to the story at hand.

Saul gave David his permissive will but he did not have his support (***Study 1Samuel 16-19***).

> ***1Samuel 18:7-9*** *And the women answered one another as they played, and said, Saul hath slain his thousands, and David his ten thousands. And Saul was very wroth, and the saying displeased him; and he said, They have ascribed unto David ten thousands, and to me they have ascribed but thousands: and what can he have more but*

the kingdom? And Saul eyed David from that day and forward.

Saul permitted David to complete the following:
- Permitted David to slay Goliath
- Chose him to live in his home and play the harp for healing purposes when the evil spirit from the Lord would oppress him
- Permitted him to marry his daughter Micah
- Permitted him to be over the men of war

Saul at times displayed acts that appeared as if he supported David:
- Saul gave David his armor when it was time to fight Goliath
- Saul loved David and made him his armorbearer
- Saul would not allow David to return home and asked his father if he could live in the palace with him

One would assume that this denoted support. Yet, when the women began to sing the song comparing Saul to David, Saul became angry and jealous. Even though he continued to use David for service, he viewed him as competition and an enemy, rather than a co-laborer in the work of God's kingdom.

When I consider Saul's challenges with David, it was evident that Saul valued David's gifts but not his identity, his calling and who he was as a person. Though all of what occurred with Saul is not my story, I can relate in that there have been an abundance of times where I felt people valued me for my gifts but not my identity, my calling – who I was as a person. I often felt and was misunderstood. Though this may have not been their heart or intent, I often experienced times where people benefited from my gifting, then they tossed me aside or ignored me until it was the next time to utilize my gifts again. I was in Holy Spirit life school and at his leading, I sought training through other ministries, read books, listened to cd's on various specialized interest that the Holy Spirit was teaching me, studied and pursued the gifts of the spirit, and was bold in activating and operating in them, etc. I then would seek to impart all of what I learned to those around me. I do not believe people knew what to do with me or what to invest into my walk. Yet, it did not lessen the pain of not being fully supported for all of who I was. I was also angry at God because I did not understand that Holy Spirit life school was cool, so in ways I felt betrayed by the same journey I loved so dearly. To me, I was left to stumble and fumble and figure it out. This did not always feel good and caused wounds in my soul and even in the foundation of my apostleship.

Due to the wounds that I incurred from my experience, I was and am determined to be a better leader and a healthy apostle that is not bound by the challenges of the journey. Even throughout my journey where I did not know I was an apostle, I would be before God sharing my hurts, anger, resentments, trials, challenges, and allowing him to heal me. I would ask for his eyes and for his compassion to see and engage people through his eyes and heart for them. This allowed me to continue his work regardless to what hurts, misunderstandings, or challenges I endured. I was able to remain balanced in not wounding others due to being wounded, and not bleeding on those I lead due to woundedness. I remember those I oversaw wanting me to display my hurt and pain and being challenged with me for continually being able to remain focused on the work at hand. As the Holy Spirit led me, I would share my hurts and concerns so that they knew I was not in denial about what was occurring to me, while using the prayer strategies God would give me to war against the doctrines and devils that challenged me and the work of the Lord. I would have them join me in prayer, and sometimes they would be challenged that we would have to war and intercede rather than handle things naturally. But we always saw great fruit from our prayers and they eventually became eager to deal with challenges in the spirit as opposed to natural means that produced little to no fruit. Moreover, God would always enable me to see what was ahead so I was able to steer those under me to the greater vision at hand. This allowed me to sacrifice my present pain for the greater glory and for the good of the full vision. I will admit that this was a daily conscious sacrifice. It was not easy as I had to keep it at the forefront of my soul and heart as if it was a part of the vision I was working on. So in public I presented as the overcomer I was, and in private, I humbled myself unto the deliverance and healing power of God.

As I came into revelation of my apostolic call, I realized that though I consistently sought God for deliverance and healing, sometimes I had to just suck it up and keep it moving. This is known as stuffing unhealthy hurts, thoughts, and feelings. It was only the grace and eyes of God, and me pursuing constant healing that allowed me to remain balanced and not eventually blow up from the volcano of pain that was in me. I therefore, have had to spend time deciphering through my apostolic journey, while seeking God to cleanse and heal my apostolic foundation and calling of unhealthy seeds, roots, and fruits that I and others planted and internally harvested. This has helped SHIFT me to journeying as a healthy apostle and provided keys for how to raise up healthy apostles, prophets, etc. I decree deliverance and healing to those who can identify with my story. That you have received healing keys from my story, that you will be healed and can learn from the trials of your journey. **SHIFT!**

Nina Cooks Journey As A Healthy Apostle
As I walk in my apostolic calling I have the privilege of being able to walk as a healed apostle. Although there are times where I need healing personally, generationally, concerning ministry, etc., I do not remain in a place of woundedness, harboring hurt, or not knowing how to pursue God for healing and truly receive it. As I walk in my calling I understand that healing is a normal part of my daily walk with the Lord, and it is okay to need healing because as a human being, challenges, issues, hurts, and wounds are inevitable. They are not meant to stay in you, form you, and dictate who you are in the Lord and who he is in you. This is something that I have had to learn because initially I felt that needing healing was a bad thing. It would make me feel like I was weak, and I would also be ashamed of the things I needed healing from. It would reveal and expose my imperfections. Sometimes if I hurt someone because I needed healing and was not resting in the process of my healing, I would completely shut down and feel extremely condemned by my actions. I would beat myself up

about it for days and weeks, and it would alter my interactions with that person and the people around me where I would be too hurt and ashamed to talk to them or interact with them. I would feel unworthy of their interaction and embrace. I would be in a state of shame, guilt and condemnation rather than realizing that needing healing is a part of life, is one of the reasons why Jesus died for us. It was so we could receive healing through him. I learned through my relationship with him, that it would be very important for me to receive him as THE HEALER and stop trying to heal myself. I recognized the need to be free from perfection, pride, shame, guilt, and condemnation; and that the areas in which I need healing just show that those are places where I need God and where his grace and power will abide if I just let go and give them to him. This took me about a year to learn, and although it was a very hard and intense year, I would not trade my life lessons for anything in the world. It changed my life, and was a very needed foundational year for the rooting and development of my apostolic calling.

Apostles need to learn how to embrace and handle healing and how to live daily lives in relationship with God as the healer. They have to know the healer intimately, and relinquish all things that would hinder them from embracing healing. It is not something to despise or degrade. As an apostle consistent deliverance and healing is something to be embraced because of the increased levels of warfare of all kinds, (e.g. regional, territorial, national) that we face. Also because of the influence and effects that apostles have over the lives of many people; I understand that in order for me to stay pure and undefiled, God-focused and God-driven in my walk, the process of continual healing is key to my ability to produce godly fruit in all of the things that God sets to my hands, in the lives of others, and in my personal life as well. After receiving this revelation and embracing a daily lifestyle of healing, I consistently walk as a healed apostle.

As I grow in my calling, become more defined, learn new things about who I am in the Lord, I step out further in who I am as an apostle. God is continually revealing to me areas where I need healing and this is now a part of the process that I have embraced. I have grown in quickly recognizing when I need healing, cleansing, and transformation. And because I have embraced healing, I can discern the necessity for it before God brings it to my attention and before others reveal it to me. I look for healing, and I am quick to say *"Oooh that needs to be healed!"* I am proactive in healing and I do not let things go undealt with and ignored with the mindset that it will take care of itself. I understand that as the governor and watchman of my own calling and destiny, I have to be the one to be accountable and responsible for adequately governing my own calling and destiny even as I govern the calling and destiny of others. If I do not know and am not skilled in my ability to handle the things that rise in the development of my calling, I will not be able to handle the calling itself. I have to be able to be an apostle within myself before I can be an apostle to others. I have to be able to personally understand my process of development as an apostle, before I can help another to develop in their calling. I have to be skilled in healing and know how to pursue, seek, and receive Gods healing for myself before I can heal somebody else.

This was all a part of things that I have learned as an apostle. Now when things are exposed to me, I am readily open to receive healing. I am in no way saying that this takes the pain out of hurts, but I am saying that what I have learned has caused me to be at peace when it comes to needing healing. It has made my process less stressful and prolonged, and more beneficial and fruitful. In times of healing I can now see why it is important for me to be healed from certain things. I can see how they can be a detriment to me, and I can see how it is forming godly character in me allowing me to receive greater definition as an apostle.

God blessed me with a spiritual mother that helped identify me as an apostle, and has been able to walk with me as I learned the healing keys needed to develop as a healthy apostle. I have partaken of the revelation and wisdom she has imparted through her apostolic journey and can apply them to my life as the Holy Spirit leads, to further fortify and heal me as an apostle. No matter how hard my life was and has been, my spiritual mother kept pushing me to embrace my calling and identity as an apostle, embrace the processing that has come with my journey, embrace deliverance and healing as a part of my lifestyle, and be okay that I am evolving as an apostle. She continually speaks truth to me, corrects and encourages me, and continually prays for me and with me, while journeying with me through my processes of healing and unfolding as an apostle. She taught me how to pursue God for healing, and gave me the skills to receiving healing. For example:

- How to pray defined prayers
- How to pray healing soaking prayers rather than warfare prayers
- How to do self-deliverance from demonic oppressions
- How to use the blood of Jesus to cleanse my soul, heart, mind, body, identity
- The importance of journaling and communing with God
- How to be honest with God and just have conversation with him
- How to study and use the scripture to be healed and empowered, and so much more

Without her identification, support, counsel, guidance, mentoring, empowerment, training, and mothering, I would not have learned these healthy keys as quickly as I did. And with the past challenges I needed deliverance and healing from, I probably would have caused harm to myself and others as I embark upon my apostolic walk. Eventually, I would have learned them on my own, but she saved me much time, challenges, and hardship by journeying with me, empowering me, and being who God called her to be in my life. She has not just been a leader in name, but in deed. Four years into my apostolic journey with the Holy Spirit and I already know how to walk as a healed apostle. And to embrace Holy Spirit leading, guiding, and molding me into the apostle Jesus has designed me to be. I have not even been publicly ordained yet. So I can just imagine how many wounds and challenges I am bypassing, and how God is going to be able to use me mightily as his healthy apostle.

UNCONFIRMED VERSUS CONFIRMED AS AN APOSTLE

Taquetta Baker's Unconfirmed Apostolic Journey

In this day and age, some saints operate as apostles, but since the office is not sufficiently discussed and embraced, they do not know they are apostles. They therefore stumble and fumble through their calling and do not have the adequate terminology, teaching, and skills to be a healthy and successful apostle. They are also defined under other terms that do not provide the authority that comes with their calling. They endure a lot of hardships and warfare from the enemy and people who are resistant to the work they are doing. Or who are resistant to the instability they may show since they do not know they are apostles.

There is another group of saints, who know they are apostles, but do not want to be rejected, viewed as prideful and haughty, or do not want the challenges, persecution, and warfare that comes with the calling so they reject it. One revelation we must be clear on is that rejecting a gift or calling does not make the gift disappear. Rejection also does not stop the devil from wreaking havoc in our lives and ministries. **Romans 11:29** *For the gifts and calling of God are without repentance.* The gift is still theirs and the devil is always messy..

I was not initially confirmed by man as an apostle. I did not know that I was an apostle and others around me and over me did not initially know. The only titled apostles I knew at the time was the main pastor of the church I attended and John Eckhardt of Chicago,

Illinois. I did not know all that it entailed, but it seemed like big shoes to fill. I was not trying to be an apostle or have any other title for that matter. For years I called myself a servant. I was a self-declared servant. I would say *"I am a servant,"* when people within the ministry or abroad would label me as a minister or prophet. I did not want any parts of a title. I did not want to fail people. Though I was a key leader within the church and within my sphere of influence, I did not want the weight and responsibility of a title. I was also ignorant to the power and authority that came with enmeshing with the title of my calling, so I did not know that refusing to embrace the title and the calling was a rejection of my power and authority. In addition, there was this negative insinuation which resonated within the body of Christ, that if you wanted a title, then you were seeking to promote yourself and to be important. I never wanted anyone to think that of me. I also witnessed how others before me recognized who they were and acknowledged it, were rebuked, rejected, and slandered for it. I definitely did not want that. Though I had pioneered a choreographed dance ministry, pioneered the Sunday morning praise and worship dance ministry, established other dance ministries throughout the body of Christ, assisted with teaching during prophetic trainings that were a trailblazing work within our church, community and sphere of influence, was the leader of the altar workers ministry and used that avenue to draw people off the pew into their giftings and callings, was a key mentor within the church and abroad, pioneered various conferences and events within the church, community, and abroad, was eventually placed on the presbytery board, taught Sunday school, preached and taught at various services within the church and abroad, wrote books, pioneered my own ministry and counseling center, etc., I was not acknowledged or mentored as an apostle, and did not know myself that I was an apostle.

After 9 or so years of attending my previous church, Jesus revealed to me during my personal prayer time that I was an apostle. He began to show me in visions how this was so and how all I had been doing was training me as an apostle. I still did not understand what that meant. I had God's word and confirmation but no clarity on what it meant to be an apostle. Around this time, leadership and the saints began acknowledging me as a prophet. I had/have never been set as a prophet minister but was being acknowledged as one. I have a prophetic gift and I sought God continually for words for people. I was always seeking to see God move. I also had seasons where God would strongly train me in different areas and this season it was the prophetic. Interestingly, others abroad begin acknowledging me as an apostle. They recognized the prophetic gift but also the mentoring, the pioneering, the trailblazing, and etc. Because God had told me I was an apostle, when people would call me a prophet, a strong conviction would come upon me if I did not correct them. God would tell me that I was not correcting them to be haughty, but simply because an apostle was who I was, and that I needed to agree with it and embrace it.

One day the Lord told me I needed to stop respecting what people could handle about me and start embracing the truth of my identity. I was like *"Whoaaaah Jesus!"* That is exactly what I was doing, I was respecting what people said, but I was challenged that they could not really see me for who I was. Yet, during this time I was very uncomfortable with stating I was an apostle, and even embracing it when those abroad acknowledged it in me. Especially since my leadership did not identify me in this capacity. I honored them and did not want to overstep any boundaries with them. I also had to be careful not to anger the Lord by being disobedient, so it was a trying season in my life. I often felt like I needed to explain my calling to people who misspoke concerning me, and that people were judging me even though they would not say anything when I corrected them. Even when I stated it, it would be through subtle rejection and shame. When people asked me what my calling was or titled me as a prophet, I would say "*God said I was an apostle.*" I blamed it all on God in hopes they would take up their charge with him and not me.

When we are unconfirmed in our identity and calling, the enemy can use shame, condemnation, rejection, and fear of man and religious perceptions to coward us from receiving the truth of who we are. **Romans 8:1** declares:

> *There is therefore now no condemnation to them which are in Christ Jesus, who walk not after the flesh, but after the Spirit.*

My apostolic works and identity were mantled in the essence of Jesus Christ, but how I embraced my calling was through the well of the flesh. I therefore, incurred shame, condemnation, rejection and fear. Had I embraced my calling, I would have been able to operate in spiritual peace and truth and not endure the negative attributes that came with being unconfirmed, as they became a part of me – a part of my mantle – a part of my identity. This would have also allowed me to embrace the reality that Jesus had confirmed me. Whose word and confirmation was more powerful than Jesus? NO ONE! I decree that you are being healed from all the challenges and condemnation that came form being unconfirmed. That you are healing in the truth that God has confirmed you and he is the ultimate authority in your life and in all the universe. ***SHIFT!***

Nina Cook's Confirmed Apostolic Journey

I was confirmed from the onset of identifying my calling, so I was able to readily accept and embrace my calling. Receiving confirmation helped me to be more confident in who I am and be shameless about it, even though I am still processing into the office of an apostle. From the onset of exploring who I was in God, the apostolic calling became established in me as truth. My apostolic calling became my foundation, and thus provided solid ground to build my identity, life, and ministries upon. I have assurance and security in who I am. I am also able to believe, receive, and trust in the calling and that it was indeed from the Lord.

I have been cultivated into apostleship like a young child who is empowered in their beauty, talent, and intellect by their parents. As they become adults they still believe that they are beautiful, talented and intelligent. Because they were confirmed in this identity, they have formed a healthy and balanced self-esteem. This is what the words of those who confirmed and encouraged me in who I am did for me. They helped to form a healthy and balanced spiritual self-esteem and spiritual identity in me. And because of this, my natural self-esteem and identity receives continual healing and healthy molding, while empowering me to come into a place of total wholeness both spiritually and naturally.

My spiritual mother was the first person to confirm me in my apostolic calling. As I am developing into the fullness of the office, she constantly mothers me in it just as the example I gave above of the parent and the child. And upon meeting those who she had walked in ministry with for years, they would quickly see who I was, and would call me out as an apostle. They would even pull on and activate the apostolic mantle upon me. They did not waste any time, they saw the calling and immediately confirmed me. They then began to establish me in the manifestation of it. Because there was so much being invested in me and so much being seen in me by others this made me want to come forth more, to learn more, to grow more, to do more and etc. Having mature leaders and ministers confirm me was very encouraging, activating, and igniting to my spirit. I looked up to them, as they were mighty apostles, prophets, teachers, prayer warriors, and demon busters. When they confirmed me, it told me that I could access the same power and abilities they had. It let me know that the sky was the limit and that truly there was nothing that I could not do in Jesus.

Being confirmed strengthened me and made me more firm in my calling. I knew that people believed in the vision of God that was on my life and that they supported it. It is one thing to see yourself and know what the Lord has said to you which is crucially important, but it is very encouraging and securing to know that other people can see you as well, and have also heard from the Lord on your behalf. Confirmation brings validation, assurance, security, approval, and empowerment. Especially when life experiences from childhood, family relationships, friends, and interactions, cause hurts in our identity and have wounded our self-image. Wounds in these areas will hinder us in our ability to receive and embrace the truth of who we are, and walk in the truth. Often times, confirmation provides healing to areas in our identity where we have not felt validated and worthy. But we cannot rest on the confirmation of others alone for the validation of who we are. In doing so, we will always be looking for the approval and acceptance of man. We need to process through inner healing in our self-esteem, self- confidence, and self-perception such that we can walk in the foundational truths about ourselves and be secure and confident in our identity. Not everyone will confirm you and that is okay. Not everyone will acknowledge you and that is okay. Stand firm in who you are, and do not allow the rejection of others to draw away from God's will for your life, and deter you from advancing in the work of the Lord. Receiving healing in these areas will help you to embrace confirmation and walk confidently in your apostolic calling.

BLIND DESTINY VISION VERSUS

CLEAR DESTINY VISION

Taquetta Baker's Blind Destiny Vision

One of my biggest challenges regarding my apostolic calling and spiritual walk in general, is that though I was raised in the church, I was never cultivated in a spiritual destiny vision for my life. Until I was in my mid 30's, I was blind to the fact that God had a destiny plan for my life. The apostolic vision for my life would prevail much later once I gained revelation of my destiny plan. Growing up I always wondered why people did the things they did. I therefore, wanted to be a counselor from a young age. By the time I was in college, I had my life planned. By age 30, I was going to get my Master's degree, get married, have children, and eventually open up a residential home for traumatized girls. At the age of 27, my life took a major spiritual turn and I ended up moving to Muncie, IN. I had only planned on staying here for five years. I was tricked here by God (real life), under the guise that I was going to help my spiritual mother with her ministry. After she was up and going, I would move to Texas where I always wanted to live. Needless to say, I am 44 years old now. I still reside in Muncie. I did get that Master's degree before I moved here and before age 30. I however, am not married, do not have any children, nor have I opened a residential home for traumatized girls. Instead of helping my spiritual mother with her ministry, I have my own ministry that raises up other ministries, businesses, and organizations, am the pastor of a church, have a counseling business, and have been called to complete a work here in the region of Muncie. I love being here now and cannot wait to return to my home and town when I travel. I did not always feel this way, for this love came with destiny vision that I incurred over time.

When I first moved to Muncie I hated it. I was used to the big city life where I had lots of friends, family support, and an abundance of opportunity. Here in Muncie everything was small though big in its own right. There was not much to do and everybody knew everybody, so there was a lot of familiarity at work. The church I attended was SHIFTING out of the Pentecostals Assemblies Of the World into the Apostolic. They had released the women to wear pants, make-up, cut their hair, and etc. Saints could not go to the movies and the like without it being a sin, etc. All of which I did and more. I was so modern that my hair was cut in a fade, I had waves, and every other week I would dye it different colors. I loved colors, was very stylish, and I matched from head to toe. I was very intelligent and had already cultivated a relationship with Jesus Christ. I therefore, studied all the time, and many of my gifts were already being cultivated in his presence, rather than being cultivated by a religious structure or school. I learned that we can desire change but reject it at the same time. Because of the rejection by those who were not ready for the change they said they wanted, not having friends, living in a small town, receiving challenges due to not being able to equate my spiritual knowledge to a natural teacher or trainer, I dreaded this SHIFT in my life. My spiritual mother was my best and only friend for years. I would say to her "*If you died, I would be alone.*" Though she is still alive to this day, I would be angered by the thought of her dying and leaving me in Muncie alone. Aside from helping my spiritual mother with ministry, I had no initial clue of my purpose in Muncie. Outside of us doing ministry together, my spiritual mother did not have vision for my SHIFT. She felt it was God for me to be here, but she did not entice me to come to Muncie, and left it up to me and Jesus regarding moving here. Though a couple of leaders felt it was God's will for me to move to Muncie, neither of them had clear vision on the purpose of my SHIFT! My aunt raised me in God, in the things of God, yet she did not tell me growing up that all this would happen. It would be years before I knew this SHIFT was God ordained and I had been set up by Jesus.

Because I had no vision, I was angry, resentful, and even emotionally rebellious at times regarding being in Muncie. I say emotionally rebellious because I was obedient to the Lord with my actions, but for years, my heart was grievous regarding the things he would have me to do. I was always talking about and seeking God for when I could move to Texas. He would refresh me, give me time away from ministry, empower me with more of his Spirit, then tell me I had to complete my work. He would then give me another assignment and I would fervently go forth in what he was saying, but equated it to me helping the church and those around me. I did not view it or understand it as kingdom vision for my life. I felt punished and trapped in the life God had chose for me. I did not understand how it could be my truth when much of life, I lived with a different vision plan. I was well liked in the state I lived in before moving to Muncie. I did not understand how God could move me to a place where people were suspicious and rejecting of me simply because I represented the very thing they said they wanted. At that time it did make sense to me. As I think on it now, my frustrations could have blocked me from seeing and clearly hearing truth or God did not tell me cause I was not ready for truth.

For several years, I shared an apartment with my spiritual mother. I would toss around the idea of getting my own home, but then would contend I would be leaving so I can just wait until I move to Texas. After a while, Jesus continued to give me more assignments. I also began to experience some breakthrough at the church I was attending. The dance ministry was being accepted and we had constant dance ministry assignments within the church and abroad. We also started a dance ministry for Sunday morning praise and worship and it was now being embraced as a necessary part of the service. I was made leader of the Altar Workers Ministry which had its initial challenges, but eventually SHIFTED where people wanted to be a part of the ministry and people would come up for prayer. I would pioneer various deliverance and healing events at the church and abroad, and we would experience lots of fruit and breakthrough from these endeavors. I did not know it at the time, but the dance ministry was like my fivefold ministry team. They would help me pioneer these events. They gave tirelessly of their time, gifts, finances, etc. They were like Nehemiah and the crew.

They did the foot work, the behind the scenes work, that no one wants to do, interceded and warred to birth the event in prayer, and then worked the event to ensure it was successful and pleasing to God. Their labor of love to God, me, and the work he granted to our hands was captivating. We were all seen as outcast but we labored in spite of it all. As I look back on it now, they were millennials who were years ahead of the righteous rebellion that is arising now in Christendom. Since we were doing all this, I thought it best that I look for a home. I figured when God does release me, I could sale the home and SHIFT to Texas. Yes Lord!

When I moved into my home, the first several years, I lived like I was their temporarily. I had all the furnishings but I had no pictures on the wall. When something broke I would immediately fix it and I would always paint and do touch ups on the wall so it was prepared for sale. Though I had always experienced lots of warfare, the warfare intensified with me obtaining my own home. I mean it was crazy. I will speak on it in another chapter. The warfare only strengthened my desire to move up out of Muncie. Yet, God kept giving me more assignments. I only wanted to be in the will of the Lord, so I would surrender and pour my life into them.

One day I was sitting in the living room and the Lord said, *"you have moved to a new home but you have to move in."* I was like *"huh Lord?"* At this time, I had been in my home for almost three years so I was confused. He then began to show me how I had no pictures on the wall and how I lived as if I was moving at any moment. I tried to appease God by getting a few pictures and trying to embrace the house more as my actual home. Of course God knows our heart so he called me out on this. This was a constant battle between God and I because the truth is God was trying to get me to embrace Muncie and we know I was NOT trying to hear all that.

As the church I was attending SHIFTED to more liberation and embracing of the apostolic, things got better for me. Since my home was very nice, baby showers, bridal showers, college bible studies, and just fun nights would occur at my home. People still did not know what to do with me or how to pour into me. Some tolerated me, while others accepted me. Toleration was better than ostracism, though both possess thin lines to being rejected and reminded at anytime that you are not elite and you are not fully accepted.

Mostly the youngens were drawn to me. This is interesting because years ago I would say *"the anointing is on those 35 and younger – we need to be equipping them in their giftings and callings, and raising them up to do the work of the Lord."* This word was continuously overlooked. I however, would use the altar workers ministry and the arts to draw the youngens off the pews. I would begin personally mentoring them in their calling even though, aside from gifts and church works, no one was really being released in their calling. At least they knew I saw and confirmed them and more importantly that Jesus saw and confirmed them. Now in 2017 we are calling these same youngens millennials. Challengingly, now we have a host of

- Millennials who are angry at the church and leaders, do not want to go to church, and are rebellious against doctrine and anything that would try to put them in a box.
- Millennials who are dying in dead churches that refuse to SHIFT the baton to them. They are so loyal they cannot get themselves to leave despite knowing they are spiritually dead and that the church is stuck, idle, and DEAD!
- Millennials who I call Nicodemuses; they sneak around the body of Christ and get their Jesus fix; they get filled up with Jesus, equipped in their giftings and calling, then sneak back into their church and sit on the pews or return to working their religious position as if they had not been anywhere.
- Millennials who are anointed but rebellious; they are starting their own ministries, yet still bound in sin, worldliness, church hurt, etc.; they put a worldly twist on the things of God then rebelliously STRIKE against the saints who call out their unrighteousness.
- Millennials who are ON FIRE FOR GOD! They know they are called and want what God has for them. Some of them have spiritual parents, mentors, and leaders who have gotten a clue and are helping them SHIFT into their identity and calling. Some of them only have Holy Spirit school teaching and guiding them. They

are stumbling and fumbling, but their hearts are pure for the Lord and the things of God.

I believe this rebellion is because of what they have witnessed in the church over the years. It is also due to the fact that they are anointed to do a work NOW, but doctrine and man have said they have to go through 20 more years to be processed, identified, and released in their calling. They were busting out the seams then. Now they are ALL EXPOSED, while declaring "WE AIN'T GOING NOWHERE!" " WE ARE HERE TO STAY!"

But let me get back to the story cause that is probably a topic for a different book.

Even with an abundance of fruit manifesting, I still viewed everything as an assignment and not a lifestyle or the actual vision plan for my life. By this time I knew I was being equipped for a greater work, but I still thought that work was in another state and that when this assignment was over, Muncie was over. Instead of that occurring, God began to give me revelation about my own ministry. This is where I began to get vision about who I was and what I was to be doing in the kingdom aside from the church. I also had insight by this time that I was an apostle even though I was not keen on declaring it from the rooftops. I was still shy about it and standing behind *"God said."* As God gave me the name of my ministry, Kingdom Shifters Ministries (KSM), and some of the vision for it, I took it to my pastors. It was the BIG picture but not all the details in between. I only had present details and a BIG picture. I sure was in for a spiritual awakening.

At this time, it would just be the name I went under as I traveled abroad preaching, teaching, pioneering, etc. I ministered in dance and taught at a lot of dance and fine art conferences, prayer, deliverance, healing, and prophetic events. I also began to mentor abroad, so all of this was through KSM. My leaders permitted me to use my ministry in this fashion. I even had a couple of people from the church who had been given permission to be a part of the ministry. After a while, God started dealing with me about successorship. I began to train people to be leaders over the ministries I was a part of in the church and eventually, I stepped down and became assistants to those ministries, while equipping the leaders to oversee them. This was a huge SHIFT because successorship was not thought of and so there was a resistance to it. Even from those who were placed in my stead. I however, had to do what God said. So I supported, trained, empowered, role modeled, and tried to impart the value of successorship in hopes that it would in time be embraced. I was traveling a lot in ministry and was only at church a couple times of month. I loved traveling as of course it was away from Muncie, and it was awesome to meet so many saints and to do an extended work in the kingdom.

One day in prayer, God began to give me more revelation about the vision of KSM. He told me he wanted me to do a monthly Holy Ghost Agenda Service in Muncie and that eventually it would become its own entity. Up until this point, all the work I did in KSM was abroad. Anything I did in town was through other churches or through the church I was in. I did not realize this and I did not grasp what "*entity*" meant until my assistant pastor questioned me on it, and wanted me to go back to God for more clarity. When going back to God I did not receive more clarity on the "*entity*" part of the vision as that came later. I did get more clarity on who I was as an apostle and what I would be doing in the region through the Holy Ghost Agenda Service. The vision of the service was to help birth consistent miracles and healing into the region. It would also be a training service that equipped people in fivefold ministry so they could take back what they learned and impart it into their church. I shared that with my co-pastor. This was all new to her, and of course new territory. Basically if they allowed me to do "Holy Ghost Agenda," it would be like an extended work of their ministry in the community. Challenges began to arise as to how to go about this. We had several meetings that examined much of my time under their covering. We learned a lot from one another in these meetings and cleared up a lot of misconception regarding experiences that occurred over the years. We decided that we would both pray as to whether they were to cover me in the new place I was in regarding KSM. As I prayed and searched God he told me that my assignment was completed and that it was time for me to transition out of the church. Mind you he said out of the church, not out of Muncie. The church was all I had known so I was excited for the transition but had mixed emotions about leaving the church. God told me that I was to completely focus on KSM and to go forward with Holy Ghost Agenda while continuing to travel abroad. After receiving confirmation of what he was speaking, I shared this with my pastors. They never shared with me their thoughts on the topic. They respected my decision and I took the proper channels and transitioned as the Lord required.

When I SHIFTED, I began to find ways to equip myself as an apostle and as a founder of a ministry. KSM had been in existence for two and a half years by then but now it was just me and Jesus and my small team who was permitted to still be a part of the ministry. I still had a lot of unresolved indifferences and challenges regarding the reason I was sent to Muncie, having to still do a work in Muncie, experiences that occurred as I was being Holy Spirit trained as an apostle, about being an apostle and what that actually meant, and with challenges that occurred while transitioning out of the church. No matter how proper you transition, leaving and losing the familiar is always trying and brings its own set of experiences, thoughts, and feelings to process through.

As I read the book, *"Spurned into Apostleship"* by Apostle Jackie Green, I began to receive answers, biblical revelation for all the things I had questions about over the years, clear vision that I was an apostle, what that generally entailed, and the reason I was sent to Muncie. After 13 years (cracking up), I learned that God hid me in Muncie to be in incubation so he could do a work in me for a greater apostolic purpose. When you are in incubation with God, you are in personal communion and intimacy with God. While there, you are inducted into Holy Spirit life school, God impregnates you with his vision for your calling and then trains you in that calling. God as well hid me to:

- Preserve me
- Decontaminate and purge me from sin and self
- Protect me from contamination of sin, demons, religion, and tradition
- Protect me from myself and me self aborting my calling
- Instill his foundation into me
- Train me
- Equip me
- Train me as a warrior
- Make me a weapon of mass destruction
- Complete a work in the region and sphere of influence I was ministering in
- Shield me until the appointed time of commissioning and release
- Cultivate and release me for his glory - only he can take credit for all I am and will become

As you ingest my journey you already grasped this revelation right? I am still laughing and shaking my head. I wish I received this revelation sooner than I did. I certainly wish I had known when I first moved to Muncie. It would have saved me a lot of trials and tribulations or at least made them more bearable. I also would have been able to embrace Muncie and the fact that I am called to this region. I believe it is so essential that we raise up the younger generation to have and pursue Godly destiny at a young age – really from the womb. We should be asking God what their life's calling and purpose is, and rather than equipping them in gifts, we should be equipping them in their calling and destiny. As I disciple, mentor, am a God mother and spiritual parent, my first priority is to identity and confirm their calling, and to help them acquire vision for who they are in God. I then begin equipping their character, nature, and identity, in what God is saying for their life. Decreeing clear destiny vision is your portion today. **SHIFT!**

Nina Cook's Clear Destiny Vision

Though I was raised in the church I came to college with a different plan for my life than what I am walking in now. I had my plan and my biological's mother's plan for my life. I did not know God had a plan for my life until my life began to take some serious SHIFTS that altered me and my biological mother's plan for my life. In college, I started to have increased back pain which hindered my ability to adequately compete and perform as a dancer. And that also began to drain the joy and fulfillment that I received from dancing. This resulted in me making changes to my degree program, where I had to minor in dance rather than major in it. Dance had been a part of my life from a young age, and now I was having to possibly choose an alternative plan rather than dancing on Broadway and joining a dance company like I had always envisioned. Through a bible study at college, I began to attend a great church and meet some people who helped me explore God's ordained vision for my life. My mentor, who was head of the Bible study along with my spiritual mother who was a leader at the church, would provoke me to explore what God really wanted to do with my life. My spiritual mother would tell me that God would not want me to dance all these years then give it up due to injury. She would say he must have a plan to use my gift of dance for his glory. As I began to seek him, I received clear vision for how God wanted to use my gift of dance, and for the fullness of my destiny journey. I was also being equipped in continually seeking the Lord in what I was to do to further advance in destiny with him. My spiritual mother, mentor, and others have come along and confirmed, empowered, and assisted me in my God ordained destiny vision.

Aside from being an apostle, part of my destiny vision is founding a production company to which has been in existence for four years and counting. Though I thought I would return to Chicago upon graduation, the Lord has required me to remain in Muncie where I am pioneering my production company and the church I am a part of. I have clear vision for the reason I am in Muncie and enjoy my destiny walk with the Lord.

With having vision for my apostolic call and the other things God has granted to my hands, I am able to prepare not just for the present, but for the future. My spiritual mother pours her life into me which also helps me to consistently walk in the vision for my life. We have spent countless hours praying into who I am as an apostle, company owner, pioneer, etc. Often I talk and share with my spiritual mother about being an apostle, and because she is also an apostle, I am able to learn and be equipped from her experiences. In having clear vision, I have been trained in seeking the Holy Spirit on what to study and how to show myself approved of my calling. I therefore am continually equipping myself in my apostolic calling.

- I do my own studies on the apostolic
- I listen to teachings, lessons, and read books on being an apostle
- I take online classes and independent studies in on the apostolic and fivefold ministries
- I even watch history channel documentaries on the apostles of the Bible, and search for information on the origin of the apostles
- I seek and receive my own revelation and insight while also hearing from and being directed by the Holy Spirit, in how all of these endeavors apply to my apostolic journey

I am able to articulate who I am in the Lord, and when he called me, so I have embraced who I am and am free to say that I am God's apostle. I have not always been this way as in times past I would be nervous to call myself an apostle. I am not yet ordained and I would fear what people would say. As I continued to grow and mature I realized that an ordination was just an outward recognition and confirmation of what should already be in your spirit. And the call was in my spirit, the cultivation was in my spirit, the work, toil and the plowing was in my spirit. I SHIFTED to knowing that it is not the ordination that makes you an apostle, it is the call of God on your life that makes you one. So I had to say to myself, *"well are you an apostle or not?"* And when I said **"YES I AM,"** I SHIFTED to being unashamed and unapologetic about it because it was just in me and was undeniable.

At the end of the day the calling cannot be hidden and the experiences that I will have as an apostle will not change if I do not acknowledge the name of who I am. The warfare will still come, the devils will still fight me, the changes will still happen, the character formation, humbling, and processes of continual dying will still unfold. It is a proclamation of my identity and an embracing of who I am such that I too am not fighting against myself, and so that the authority and power that comes through the seal and authorization of the office will help thrust and empower me through it.

I understand God's order, so I do not just go around yelling that I am an apostle, but I know who I am and am not afraid to tell it. In this season of my life God has me hidden and protected within the ministry that I am in. I do know that once I am released into the fullness of my apostolic calling that everyone will not receive me as an apostle and that their will be experiences of rejection. But because the development of who I am as an apostle was done in an atmosphere of acceptance rather than rejection and with clear vision, my identity will be rooted and grounded enough to where I will not be moved, discouraged or deterred by rejection. Rejection will have no place in me or my apostolic identity. And through what I have learned from my spiritual mother, I will know how to handle rejection with integrity, honor, and godly character while at the same time still doing the work of the Lord and advancing his kingdom.

This is the reason it is so important to seek God for the spiritual parents, mentors, and leaders that he has specifically purposed and designed for your life. They will be able to see who you are and help guide you in the clear vision of the Lord for your life. They will not reject it, mistreat it, or abuse it. They will readily accept it because they know who they are to be in your journey, and that their womb has been chosen to help birth you into all God is requiring. With this understanding comes a love much like that of a natural parent. A nurturing love, a protective love, an unconditional love, a love to see you grow, develop, succeed and excel. From this place they will pour endlessly and tirelessly into you so that you can become the fullness of who you are to be. Not every leader or mentor you have will be like this, but it is very essential to seek God for who this person or people are in your life, as they will be abundantly beneficial in the healthy development of who you are. They will have vision for who you are and will see you years and years beyond what you can see for yourself. And because they have clear vision for who you are they will be able to see how your destinies and journeys connect. They will not be intimidated, jealous, abusive, manipulative, and angry about who you are. They will nurture your development because as you go forward, they also go forward, and as they go forward, you go forward. As an apostle it is healthy to be cultivated and developed in an atmosphere of acceptance and clear vision, such that your position in your own identity and calling is one where you accept and embrace yourself. Also so that rejection and blindness does not enmesh itself in your calling, while aiming to become a part of you.

Although apostles have to deal with a lot of rejection and operate in blind faith with the Lord. This blind faith is not blind vision. We are meant to go forward in clear vision and persevere in the sight of the Lord.

JOY VERSUS TOLERATION OF
THE APOSTOLIC JOURNEY
Taquetta Baker's Journey of Toleration

Initially, I tolerated my apostolic journey. Though I had lots of moments of laughter, fond memories that I will always cherish, enjoyable successes that came from the works of my journey, I did not have true and complete joy in my apostolic journey. I lacked identity and destiny vision, so many times I operated through obedience and the fact that I could not see myself living any other life. We often quote the scripture that obedience is better than sacrifice (*1Samuel 15:22*). This makes obedience seem very matter of fact. But obedience is not just a physical act of harkening unto the voice and will of God. It is a spiritual act and posture. It is a matter of the heart. No matter what our actions are, God knows our heart. He knows if our heart is really obedient and submitted to him or if we are just putting in works. Sacrifice in the scripture is actually a physical act of offering something up to the Lord as an act of worship. I would equate sacrifices that we do because we have to and not because we want to as works rather than worship. It is a fleshly act of working for the Lord but not worship unto the Lord. If our heart is not postured in obedience then we can very well be offering God a sacrifice of works while contending it is obedient worship. I believe I was guilty of this at times. I believe God granted me grace because I did not have a plan B, I did not pursue a plan B, and I did not want a plan B. I could not imagine my life anywhere other than the will of God and I refused to yield to anything that was not of God. This did not make my actions right. I was very wrong. Yet, being sold out kept God from harshly judging me or even stripping me of my mantle due to my heart not being completely postured in obedience.

God may have also granted me grace because he knew I was being trained as an apostle, and in due time I would come into my identity, vision, and the complete joy of my apostolic calling. As I partook of the *"Spurned into Apostleship"* book, I began to learn so much about myself as an apostle that it invigorated me with joy. It was an awakening of finally know who I was, why I was, and what I shall continually unfold to be. One chapter talks about the importance of declaring out loud who you are as an apostle, and how you must declare it with your life, your words, and actions. My life and actions were speaking, but my words were still whispering. The book states the following:

> *When these three line up there is going to be a profound release upon your life and in the lives of others. Make a public declaration to people, principalities and powers in the region and thirdly in public action or demonstration that may include a name change, a title change with a change in structure and ministry vision. This is not for flaunt but principalities respond to the authority and rank in a declared name!*

I love to beat the devil down so I think declaring it to the devil is what got me most hyped about having an encounter where I truly embraced my apostolic call.

The book also states that when we decree and embrace our apostolic calling, our name is SHIFTED in the spirit realm and to regions.

> *A name change is a decree to a region and atmospheric realms and of course to people. There is power and authority in a name if God changes your name! It's God's signature and trademark upon our lives.*

As I read this I was ready to SHIFT. I therefore stood up bellowing to the top of my lungs, I decreed who I was to people, principalities and the like and *Whewww*! I had a divine encounter where a weight was lifted off of me and a newness came over me. Also a clearing of gloom, depression, and darkness cleared from around me and never returned. It was so liberating and transforming until I kept yelling **"I AM AN APOSTLE!"** and started texting it to people! In that instance I was reminded of an experience I had a few days earlier where I was called out at a service to come up and pray, and while doing so, the speaker asked "what is your title and I said "God said I am an apostle." After the services, I was challenged by a religious spirit who let me know they were an apostle even though they do not tell anyone. She then proceeded to question and try to get me to prove to her that I was an apostle. Yet, others were coming up referring to me as apostle as they made reference to the prayer I prayed. The signs and wonders was speaking for me that day. I was then reminded of another instance where I revealed that God said I was an apostle when teaching and the assistant pastor quoted me in his message during the service. It was like his words pierced the atmosphere like a sharp knife. But now I was the sign and the wonder. Now I was the sharp knife. I was decreeing it in first person for the first time. Not standing behind God. Not fearing man. And blasting principalities and powers with my identity. It was a whole new revelation, liberation, and excitement. And the beginning of true joy entering my apostolic journey.

> ***Isaiah 45:19 The Amplified Bible*** *I have not spoken in secret, in a corner of the land of darkness; I did not call the descendants of Jacob [to a fruitless service], saying, Seek Me for nothing [but I promised them a just reward]. I, the Lord, speak righteousness (the truth – trustworthy, straightforward correspondence between deeds and words); I declare things that are right.*
>
> ***The Message Bible*** *I don't just talk to myself or mumble under my breath. I never told Jacob, 'Seek me in emptiness, in dark nothingness.' I am GOD. I work out in the open, saying what's right, setting things right.*
>
> ***New Living Translation*** *I publicly proclaim bold promises. I do not whisper obscurities in some dark corner. I would not have told the people of Israel to seek me if I could not be found. I, the LORD, speak only what is true and declare only what is right.*

From this day forward, I was able to state I was an apostle even though I was still being unveiled and gaining insight into the fullness of my identity. Even with warfare and the continual deliverance and healing I was needing due to my past and the SHIFTS that were occurring in my life, I began to enjoy my spiritual walk, and was able to teach others how to enjoy their journey with God. Now I walk with God because I want to, not because I have to, and I have embraced my apostolic calling as a lifestyle.

Having covering that knows who I am in God and can impart into me also empowers me with joy. When I need wisdom, guidance, clarity, and support, she is right there. She will call or email me with words from the Lord. She sows materials into my life to help equip me in my apostolic call. She visits and spends hours training me and my team in the apostolic. She gives me opportunities and platforms to walk in my calling, while helping me plant, plow, and build my ministry. Oh yeah, that "*entity*" that I discussed in the previous chapter regarding the Holy Ghost Agenda Service, it was a church plant. Well more like an empowerment center where people are saved, delivered, healed, discipled, trained, equipped, empowered, and mentored in their calling and destiny. It is a lot of work but I LOVE MY EMPOWERMENT CENTER! I am enjoying my journey. Decreeing a SHIFT will occur in your identity where you enjoy your calling and that the joy only increases as you journey with God.
SHIFT!

Nina Cook's Joyous Apostolic Journey

There is a joy that I have about my calling and discovering more about who I am in the Lord because through mentoring and training I receive continual empowerment and encouragement to go forward. I have a safe environment to step out and try new things that God leads me to, and I fly and excel because I am given a chance to soar in what God has already placed in me. If I make a mistake I am given constructive criticism and guidance on how to improve, so I am not fearful of taking risks and chances in things that I have never done before to grow in my calling. I have access to direction and guidance, so as I step forward in what God is leading me to, I can ask questions, seek help concerning it, and have those in my life who speak into my potential to help me bring it into reality. I am excited about the things of God, about going forward even if I do not know something, and walking in who I am even if it has not been fully developed yet because I feel empowered in who I am. I have a joy about learning and being able to feast on knowledge.

My calling is something that I have accepted as my lifestyle, and I have learned how to do this through the example of the lifestyle of my leader. I have an example of what it looks like to live fulfilled in my calling, and have been taught about the importance of walking with the Holy Spirit as a friend, how to be content where God has me and what he is doing in me even if it is challenging, how to rest in God and his strength and not my own, and how to receive what I am needing from the presence of the Lord. Because I have learned how to be at peace with the lifestyle of my calling, I understand its purpose, and have completely sold myself to the calling. I enjoy my life and journey in the Lord because I know that there is no other way that I would rather live, and nothing can satisfy me like Jesus. In the ministry that I am a part of the culture is empowering and encouraging, so as I am developing as an apostle I am being cultivated in an atmosphere that is healthy and beneficial to my calling, rather than one that opposes me as I aim to grow. I am also fueled with joy in my journey to keep going forward because as I do ministry I can see the fruit of it manifest. And it is encouraging to see that even though I have not been in ministry for a great amount of years, because I have sold myself to the vision of God for my life and am constantly allowing him to teach me and grow me, fruit of that shows forth each time I do the work of the Lord.

COVERING, MENTORING &

TRAINING IN THE APOSTOLIC
Taquetta Baker's Insightful Revelation

Though Holy Spirit will be your life long mentor as an apostle, mentoring from leaders is very important and essential to becoming a healthy, balanced, successful apostle, and successfully navigating and accepting the spiritual training Holy Spirit takes you through to equip you as an apostle.

I did not initially know I was an apostle nor was I mentored in the apostolic. I would have seasons where God would train me in different gifts and offices. For several seasons I would be trained as a prophet, then an evangelist, then a teacher, etc. Just when I would feel as if I had a grasp on my calling, the season would change and another level of training would unveil. In every season, the common theme of pioneering and trailblazing ideas, movements, works and ministries, mentoring, and equipping others was evident. I would also have constant warfare that no one around me could understand or help me overcome. And many equated the warfare to sin and open doors though I was not in sin and had been in constant warfare and intercession to close up doors and cleanse my life and generational line. Had someone strategically identified, interceded, examined, trained, equipped and mentored me in my calling and not just focused on my gifts, I would have bypassed a lot of hardship and warfare that I endured with stumbling upon my calling.

In 2013, I met Apostle Jackie Green and joined her Apostles In The Making Program (AIM). I was clear that I was an apostle, but I was very wounded and needed training in my apostolic walk.

Being mentored and trained in the apostolic under the AIM program walked me through deliverance and healing. It also

- Provided further clarity, definition, revelation and identity to my experiences and my apostolic calling
- Confirmed, ordained, established, and released me through the "*sent one*" mandate
- Empowered me with revelation on the authority and power I needed to tower over the principalities and powers that were fighting against me
- Equipped me to face and handle the challenges I faced as a pioneer, trailblazer, mentor, and equipper of ministries, regions, and of the generations

Even though God told me he would send covering, and I had temporary covering when I left my previous ministry, I was not trying to hear anything about covering. And because people were speaking curses regarding me failing, I was wounded and was suspicious of having anyone over me and my ministry. I kept saying God is my covering. I even did an entire biblical study on God being my covering. I had all the biblical reasons why I did not need man to be my covering. But God knew what I needed and supplied me with the covering that I needed through Apostle

Green. The best gift Apostle Green initially gave me was that she saw I was wounded and she did not try to immediately fix my wounds, negate my wounds, demand I get over it, and force covering and mentoring on me. She was clear in what God had told her about me and who God told her she was to me, and then she said, *"but you take your time as we are just going to walk it out together."* God had informed her that she was to mentor me in the apostolic, ordain me after I completed the AIM program, that she was my spiritual mother ,and that we would do life and ministry together. Initially other than joining AIM, God had not spoken anything to me so I was giving her the wide eye. I already had a great spiritual mother so I was not sure the reason I needed another one. I tested her words constantly as we journeyed together in building a relationship. Because she met me where I was, I was able to embrace walking in the process with her and able to embrace a lasting covenant relationship that God had given us, even having another spiritual mother.

Covering, mentoring & training is important because it provides:

- Accountability
- Correction
- Counsel
- Wisdom
- Guidance
- Confirmation
- Deliverance and healing of past and present wounds

- Keeps you doctrinally sound
- Keeps you God focused & submitted to God being the head of the vision, your calling, and your life
- Fortification, support, & prayer against warfare & life challenges
- Undergirding & hands on assistance with carrying, planting, plowing, & building your apostolic walk & ministry vision
- Training and equipping
- A safe place to learn, make mistakes, & grow
- An unconditional display of the love, grace, compassion, & refuge of God
- Fresh prophecy, insight, & enlightenment of vision
- Empowerment to consistently walk in your destiny vision
- Reintegration & confirmation of the work of the Lord, navigation of changes & shifts necessary in your apostolic walk or ministry vision

Mentoring, training, and covering adds to my apostolic journey. It does not take the place of Holy Spirit life school as it is still very much me, Jesus, and Holy Spirit. Decreeing God connects you to apostolic mentoring and covering that can identify, mentor, train, equip, and empower you in your apostolic journey. **SHIFT!**

Nina Cook's Insightful Revelation

When I accepted who I was as an apostle I had already been in a place of receiving training, it just helped me value training and equipping as part of my apostolic journey. I am in a constant state of training and equipping, and I believe I will always be in training and unfolding as an apostle until I go to heaven. I live daily with a ready and open spirit to learn, and this has even infiltrated into my natural life as well. Training is not easy and has its challenging experiences. Most often, I feel that I am being trained in multiple areas at once. Sometimes I feel like I just want to focus on one thing but I cannot. I am always led to do more, while simultaneously working on what I was already doing. I recognize that this is a part of the apostle's mantle. My spiritual mother is able to encourage and pray for me so that I do not feel overwhelmed, or put unnecessary pressure on myself as truth is – it is a lot to bear at times. It is great to have her encouragement and prayer covering through my challenging or just busy seasons of training. It helps to keep me focused and aligned in healthiness and balance.

Through personal prayer and mentoring, I am able to identify what areas I am being trained in so that I can be actively engaged in what I am learning, to ensure I learn every little lesson, and receive every little intricate piece of knowledge I am to gain in that season. I do not like to miss anything because I am go getter. I like to grab ahold of the training, learn, and then walk in it successfully. At times this has caused me to walk in the spirit of perfection rather than in the spirit of excellence. Therefore, I am continually learning how to rest in the seasons of training, trust God through them, and allow the season to take its course in my life. Through my spirit of excellence I can still be actively engaged in the training, but I am not working in my own strength or with the mindset that I have to get it right or I have failed. I can rest in the peace that because I am going through the training and the Holy Spirit is producing his fruit in me, there is no way I can fail. It is not that failure is not an option, it is just that with the Holy Spirit failure does not exist.

Our apostolic training is not reading a book, going to classes, and taking test. It is training that evolves through your family, your relationships, your job, your finances, your schooling, your household, your sleep realm, your ministry assignments, and through your prayer time. It entails being trained through every day life experiences and circumstances. If these training tasks are not handled correctly, they can effect your life and the lives of others. It is hands on daily Holy Spirit training.

When the Holy Spirit enrolls me into another season of training I am able to receive support, guidance, and equipping from my leader. We need those who are committed to walk with us through our seasons of training as they help to encourage us, guide us, pray for us, and further equip us by their investment in our walk. One of the greatest benefits of having a mentor is that I am able to glean from her walk and be prepared for what is ahead. I am equipped with how to handle different obstacles and tasks with integrity and balance.

Training armors you and girds you with strength, fortification, and weaponry for present and future endeavors. Your success in training is what will determine your level of success in public ministry.

Because of the private preparation and investing into my apostolic journey from my mentor, there is an anointing of acceleration upon me. She always tells me that what has taken her years to learn takes me only months and seasons to learn. I can learn one thing on Thursday and by Sunday I am up doing it. She can pray for me for something at 5am and by 8am I am already doing it, and this is because of the mentoring that I have access to and the impartations that I have received.

As different seasons of training end and others begin, the previous training does not become just a figment of the past, it has become a part of my mantle and identity. The trainings just continue to build and build and what I have learned before, assists me in the new things that I am learning while aiding me to rest in my new season. It builds a foundation of maturity in you for the next dimensions of training and equipping that God SHIFTS you into.

FIGHTING THE GOOD FIGHT OF FAITH

As an apostle your lifestyle is war. Your literally essence - core is war as you are a weapon of destruction for God's glory.

> **1Timothy 6:12** *Fight the good fight of faith, lay hold on eternal life, whereunto thou art also called, and hast professed a good profession before many witnesses.*

We learn from this passage of scripture that because we are called as apostles, the devil will contend against us. He will combat us so that we do not want to be apostles. He wants us to shun and reject our apostolic profession, while aborting our covenant walk with the Lord.

<u>Fight</u> in the Hebrew is *agōnizomai* and means:
1. to struggle, literally (to compete for a prize) figuratively (to contend with an adversary), or genitive case (to endeavor, to accomplish something): — fight, labor fervently, strive
2. to enter a contest: contend in the gymnastic games, to contend with adversaries, fight
3. metaph. to contend, struggle, with difficulties and dangers
4. to endeavor with strenuous zeal, strive, to obtain something

This definition lets us know that we should not be waring for the sake of waring. There is a prize to obtain and an a specific purpose to be accomplished. This definition also lets us know that though we are fighting from a position of victory that Jesus won through the works of the cross, we will exert ourselves, we will labor, struggle, experience adversity, difficulties, and dangers. The devil and his imps are trying to lay claim to what is already rightfully ours. We therefore, must assert our right to have dominion over our restored inheritance, while equipping and empowering others in their dominion in the earth.

> ***Genesis 1:28*** *And God blessed them, and God said unto them, Be fruitful, and multiply, and replenish the earth, and subdue it: and have dominion over the fish of the sea, and over the fowl of the air, and over every living thing that moveth upon the earth.*

As I have sought to close generational doors, cleanse my generational line of familiar spirits and curses, and have sought to gain clarity of some of my experiences in life and with the demonic realm, it is also important to note that some of the warfare an apostle experiences can be generated from their generational lineage. I have learned through prayer and conversations with family members that the reason I am able to astral project into the spirit is because of witchcraft and idolatry practice in my family life. Also someone in my lineage dedicated the gifts and callings to the devil. Though the destiny killing spirit has tracked me from conception, as I begin to walk in my calling, attacks in the spirit realm manifested as the devil felt he had a legal right to me because of this dedication. I had to break these dedications and close up demonic portals and gateways that had been opened by generational witchcraft.

This knowledge also reveals how God uses me in the spirit and the reason I have encounter the demonic forces and witches to the degree that I have. They are familiar with my lineage and now I am familiar with them, and have learned how to conquer and resist their wickedness. You too will have a unique part of your calling that is strategic to your generational lineage. The enemy will use this as a door to war against you. As you continue to read this book, you will learn how to shut generational doors and tower over the enemy.

I have experienced warfare from the womb. I was warring for the right to exist, be born, and walk in destiny. At birth, I was waring for identity, connection, a sense of belonging, acceptance, and generational inheritance. My biological mother became pregnant with me in college. When she begin to show signs of pregnancy, she stop coming home for visits. She was not ready to be a mother, When she went into labor, she tried to give me up for adoption. The doctor recognized my mother because my great grandmother was a midwife in the area. He therefore, called her, and much convincing that her granddaughter had indeed had a child, she came to see about me. My mom still wanted to give me up for adoption. My great grandmother called my aunt who lived in New York at the time. She agreed to raise me but could not come get me for two weeks. For two weeks I was without a name. My great grandmother took me home with her and in two weeks my aunt visited. She claimed me, named me, and raised me.

Growing up I experienced constant warfare in my sleep. I would have horrible nightmares and demonic visitation. I would wear socks on my hands because my hands would be scared from hitting the bed post and walls. I would sleep with the light on at times, because of what was lurking in the dark. As I grew up, the attacks increased. By the time I was in college, I would literally have days of staying up at night to avoid the nightmares and demonic visitations. I had developed a skin disorder in my teens due to fear and anxiety, such that I would itch uncontrollably. The itching would worsen at night. Between the itching and the demons, I was being tormented. After some serious partying, risky and vile living in my early 20's, I decided to truly give my life to the Lord. Despite the foul living, I would consistently attend church, read my word, pray, and listen to christian music. The weight of living two lives and fear of something bad happening to me due to my lifestyle, SHIFTED me to giving my life completely over to Jesus.

When wholeheartedly converting unto salvation, the attacks in my sleep became more severe. I would have nightly visitations where demons would visit me and physically attack me. I would be held down, suffocated, drug out my bed. I would physically fight demons that no one could naturally see, but physically I would have bruises from being hit, beat up, and held down. I would experience sexual molestation and rape when I tried to go to sleep, or demons would try to impart things into me while I am sleep.

After moving to Muncie, the warfare intensified times ten and some, and worsened as I was being trained in the apostolic via Holy Spirit life school. In addition to what I was already experiencing, I would have soul travelers, witches and warlocks tracking me and then physically attacking me, molesting, and raping me as I slept. There have been times where I would have legions of demons walking on my roof and trying to get in my house. I would have to immediately pray against them infiltrating and they would leave. I remember one time my God brother and sister coming to pray for me and over my home. My God brother saw legions of demons over my bed. After he prayed, legions of angels surrounded my bed and home.

Demons would track me as I traveled. They would attempt to concoct assignments with other demons in the region. I would actually see these watcher and tracker spirits as I traveled in the car and on airplanes. They would be flying in the sky over me. I would see them in my yard and hear them as I would be walking to various places.

I learned that dreams were real realms, as familiar spirits, demonic agents, shape shifting demons, and witches/warlocks would enter my dream realm. One minute all would be well in the dream and the next I would be getting attacked by these entities inside my dreams, and even physically as I slept. When I would explain this, people would say I was having nightmares. I was not having nightmares. When I was a kid I was having nightmares. Spirits of terror where attacking me in my sleep. In my adult years, I was experiencing the woes of high ranking demons and witches and warlocks in my dreams. It was crazy and difficult to explain. I use to be scared to share this information for fear of being labeled as crazy. That was until I joined the AIM program and Apostle Green shared her encounters with the hounds of hell and witches. It finally had someone who could relate to what I was experiencing. Although my experiences were more extreme than hers. It was nice to know that I was not crazy and that this was due to the calling on my life.

I am very sensitive to the spirit realm. Since my youth, I could astral project into the spirit realm, especially while I was sleep. Though I can control this now through the leading of the Holy Spirit, in times past, I would wake up in the spirit realm and demons, witches, warlocks, and soul projectors would see the light of God around me and immediately fight me. Then they would visit me at night and attack me after tracking me back to my home.

Initially this was very trying warfare for me. I hated warfare. I hated the constant fighting and having to constantly cleanse and heal my soul, heart, mind, emotions, and body from the demonic impartations and wounds. I would also experience wounding from those who did not understand my warfare. They would speak things over me that brought condemnation. It would also increase my warfare as the attacks would worsen. It was as if the enemy was angry because I was seeking help, or he was using the condemnation and the words of error as an open door to further attack me.

Due to pioneering and trail blazing, some of my attacks came from being affiliated with and doing work at the church I belong to, minister abroad, and the regions and sphere of influence I was connect to. The warfare was also compounded by the resistance of those who spoke and combated against the apostolic change that God was doing within the church. I know all to well what Paul meant when he said we are was pressed on every side. I was pressed by the saints and demonic forces.

Despite the extreme warfare, God would/does give me strategic dreams and visions during my sleep and prayer time concerning how to defeat principalities and powers. I would have key information regarding the following:
- How to conquer demonic forces that attack our church and the saints
- Foreknowledge of attacks that would come to hinder ministry events and how to stop them
- What principality and powers where in the region myself and others where ministering in and how to displace them
- Foresight on present and future strategies needed to continue planting, plowing, building, and advancing the work of the Lord
- Keys for deliverance and healing of stubborn strongholds that broke people, ministries, and regions free
- Scripture revelation, new revelation, new breakthrough teachings to SHIFT and transform people and atmospheres
- Revelation for ministry assignments, dances, teachings, preaching, etc. This would be so keen that I would literally see the ministry before it occurred, knew who to minister to, what they looked like, what to wear, etc.

Often God translated me in the spirit to combat principalities or powers, complete ministry assignments, etc. The devil did not want me to sleep or to pray because he did not want me to receive this information, or to do an extended work for the kingdom. I did not know that then so I dreaded this part of my walk.

As I had accepted my apostolic calling, I also had a SHIFT of understanding my authority. I attended a deliverance conference where Apostle Ivory Hopkins was teaching. He is a general in the area of deliverance and warfare. I went up for prayer and share about the extreme warfare I was having. I thought he was going to cast the devil out of me. He said: *Daughter I need you to help me cast the devil out of these people. These demons, witches and warlocks are fighting you because of the call on your life. Until you embrace that warfare is a part of your calling and start beating them down, they will keep hounding you. Now come over hear and help me deliver these people.*

I was very relieved that I did not have a demon cause I was convinced all my self-deliverance was not working. But the thought of embracing warfare was interesting. I then read in the *"Spurned Into Apostleship"* book about knowing your rank and authority in the spirit. This was around the time that I was bellowing out that I was an apostle, so the SHIFTS in my identity were coming fast. And figuring out how to maneuver through them was interesting too.

As I begin to search out the information I was receiving, God revealed to me that I needed to be offensive in warfare. The concept of warfare being apart of my lifestyle as an apostle was new to me. I also had such extreme experiences, I was not sure I wanted this to be my norm. I wanted the warfare to cease, yet approaching it from that posture only increased the warfare. I begin to study what it meant to be offensive in warfare.

I learned that as christians we are not offensive or defensive. We are complacent. We wait on the devil to attack then we react. We actually fear rattling the devil. We deem this as ignorant, cocky, and dangerous. Yet the enemy roams the earth seeking to devour us. And even though we are to be taking the kingdom by force, and asserting dominion over the earth, we tiptoe around the earth trying to avoid the devil. The devil has been given free reign to roam. He is great at his mandate and has spewed darkness everywhere. We are bound to run into a devil and evil on a daily basis. At some point this has to stop being our approach to the enemy, especially as apostles. We must be looking for him like he is looking for us.

On defensive we should be stopping our opponent from their attack.

On the offensive we attack our opponent, while gaining leverage or victory before being attacked.

Dictionary.com defines *offensive* as:
1. making attack, aggressive, of, relating to, or designed for attack, to be irritating or annoying,

angering
2. giving painful or unpleasant sensations, nauseous, obnoxious
3. causing displeasure or resentment
4. the position or attitude of aggression or attack: an aggressive movement or attack
5. attempting to score or one up your opponent
6. disrespectful, insulting; displeasing

Synonyms for offensive: abhorrent (detestable, utterly opposed), abusive, annoying, biting, cutting, detestable, disagreeable, discourteous, distasteful, dreadful, embarrassing, evil, foul, ghastly, grisly, gross, hideous, horrible, horrid, impertinent, insolent, invidious (hateful or unfair discrimination, injurious), irritating, nauseating, objectionable, obnoxious, odious (causing hatred), off-color, offending, opprobrious (shameful or bring reproach), outrageous, repellent, reprehensible, repugnant, repulsive, revolting, rotten, rude, shocking, stinking, terrible, uncivil, unmannerly

As you can see being offensive literally means offending the devil. It means harassing, abusing, and appalling him just like he does to us. Whewwwwww! Once I got that revelation in my spirit…WHEWWWW! Along with the strategies, revelations and insight I was already receiving from the enemy, it was an entirely different war experience between me and the enemy.

I started to go bed expecting to encounter the devil.

- Before I went to bed, I would pray against the devil as God led me.
- I would use the strategies he gave me, along with the warfare weapons I had learned over the

years.
- I would send all kinds of destruction to his camp and to witches and warlocks that were attacking and tracking me. I would liken my prayers to that of King David. Since the enemy and wickedness had not grace concerning me, I had none for them.
- I would call on the angels to join me in warfare and release assignments to them as the Lord led.
- I would declare out who I was as an apostle and my authority as an ambassador of Christ, a gatekeeper of the region, and a daughter of God.
- I would declare that whether sleep or awake, I had power over the enemy. I commanded and trained my spirit to be active and alert while I was sleep and in my dreams. So even though I was asleep, my inner man would be dialoging with my spirit as I sleep. I became so keen in operating in warfare as I slept, that I knew when a demon, witch, astral projector, etc., entered my bedroom, and could discern when demons where about to attack me in my dreams. If they entered my room, I would wake up before they attacked and attack them. If they attacked in my dreams, I would gain control over the dreams and attack them. I would in essence change the dream as I attacked and what the enemy meant for bad became his own mantle of shame and destruction.
- The Bible tells us to suffer a witch not to live (*Exodus 22:18*). For some reason we do not like to pray these kinds of prayers. But witches where trying to kill me. I did/do grant them some grace in that I command them to repent, turn and serve God or die. I also threaten to cut

their silver cord as this is how they and astral projectors travel in the spirit. If their cord is cut they will die. They run quickly when you threaten to cut their life source.

Ecclesiastes 12:6-7 The Message Bible Or ever the silver cord be loosed, or the golden bowl be broken, or the pitcher be broken at the fountain, or the wheel broken at the cistern. Then shall the dust return to the earth as it was: and the spirit shall return unto God who gave it.

- I begin to command my soul to remain in my body and declare over myself that I would only travel in the spirit as the Holy Spirit led. I would decree that as the Holy Spirit led me, would be sensitive to him training me and guiding me in every assignment. I received a prophetic word that God was releasing a scepter to me in the spirit. Timothy received this word from Paul concerning prophecies spoken over him.

1Timothy 1:18 Timothy, my son, here are my instructions for you, based on the prophetic words spoken about you earlier. May they help you fight well in the Lord's battles.

I begin to decree out my prophecies and use them as weapons against the enemy. The prophecies concerning my authority in God and towering over the enemy started to manifest. I started to see my scepter during warfare and intercession, and as the Holy Spirit would lead me in the spirit realm. Night after night I would be implementing my offensive strategy and asserting my authority against the enemy. The attacks lessened and now only occur every now and again. For the most part there is a peace and clearing in my sphere of influence. Most often, am also able to discern the enemy's tactics and thwart them before he attacks or overcome him quickly if he gets one over on me. I do have to be very watchful when I travel as the enemy will try to come at me through different regions. I always have to pray over the area where I sleep, and assert my authority against principalities, powers, witches, that would try to attack me. I am offensive and war against this before I go and when I immediately enter a region. This helps me to govern the spirit realm and thwart the challenges of the enemy. I also will have my team and supports praying to further fortify me. Being offensive helps us assault the enemy rather than him devouring me.

I pray my testimony is not scaring you. I also do not wish to astonish you with wild stories. My heart is to express that apostolic warfare is real and that even if you do not have warfare as intense as mine, you have to be fierce and fearless against the enemy.

I still experience other kinds of warfare that the average apostle endures. As I have learned my identity as a warring apostle, I also pursue the devils and wickedness so I am constantly at war. I have embraced it as a part of my calling and for the most part, I am at peace with beating the devil down.

Another key that I have learned is that the enemy will operate illegally against the apostle. We have been religiously taught that all his attacks are due to us having sin and open doors, or God's permissive will.

The apostles were doing the work of the Lord when they experienced continuous persecution and warfare. The only open door they had was being called of God. Even when the girl was following Paul and the others around proclaiming that they were the servants of the most high God (*Acts 16:17*), she spoke truth, but was harassing them with it.

> *Acts 16:17-18 The same followed Paul and us, and cried, saying, These men are the servants of the most high God, which shew unto us the way of salvation. And this did she many days. But Paul, being grieved, turned and said to the spirit, I command thee in the name of Jesus Christ to come out of her. And he came out the same hour.*

<u>Grieved</u> in this passage is *diaponeōrom* and means:

1. to toil through, i.e. (passively) be worried: — be grieve
2. to work out laboriously, make complete by labour, to exert one's self, strive
3. to manage with pains, accomplish with great labour
4. to be troubled, displeased, offended, pained, to be worked up

The spirit in this girl was illegally grieving, tormenting, draining, offending, and afflicting Paul and his team. The grief was causing them to labor more than they needed to bring breakthrough. Paul became weary of this and cast the spirit out of the girl.

Please understand that your authority will increase and you will have apostolic jurisdiction over your sphere of influence, but the warfare is inevitable. There will always be devils contending against the work you are doing for the Lord. This does not mean you are not maturing or asserting you rank and authority as an apostle. It just comes with the calling and mantle that is upon your life. Some of the warfare I endure now is as followed:

- Mind binding and mind blinding spells, incantations, mind control, and telepathy where thoughts, signals and devices are sent to bind and block my ability to receive insight, visions, and revelations from God.
- Demonic oppression, rejection, and hinderances in all sorts of capacities, even from the church and those I was doing ministry with.
- Attacks on my finances, my loved ones, team members; attacks on my name.
- Mind attacks on my identity and ability to do what God called me to do.
- Floods of vile tormenting thoughts when I am about to minister even if it is a small assignment. It will be thoughts about matters God has already healed me of -that I have already overcome. Or things to try to reestablish offense, cause offense, or to steal my focus from praying and resting in the assignment at hand.
- Depression and heaviness from the region that is sent to discourage, distract, or hinder me.
- A lot of negative chatter from the demonic realm and people sent to grieve and discombobulated me.
- Dishonor from people, ministries, and demons operating against my calling and the work God is leading me to do.
- Warfare from principalities and powers within

the region or regions I minister in that do not want to be displaced.
- Constant spiritual battles over my womb spiritually and naturally. This is in effort to abort the apostles and prophets I am to birth, nurture, and mentor spiritually and naturally. And an attempt to kill the visions God is birthing through my womb.
- Constant afflictions that doctors cannot cure, and do not have any personal or generational basis.

Much of this warfare is dismantled by rebuking the enemy. Nevertheless it is annoying and like Paul expressed, aggravating. I decree that you SHIFT to knowing that the weapons of your warfare are not carnal but mighty through God for the pulling down of strongholds. I decree that you recognize that no weapon formed against you is prospering. They are eternally annihilated as you assert your rank and authority to tower over devils and have dominion in the earth. **SHIFT!**

Nina Cook's Good Fight Of Faith

The apostolic career is one of warfare. There are continual bouts of warfare that the apostle goes through because of the calling that is on their lives and the nature of the work that they are called to do. I learned this very early on in the journey of my calling and I was even taught strategic ways that the enemy attacks. I have been prepared in what to expect so when I encounter certain attacks, I can identify what is occurring and how to counterattack them. Through training I have become skilled at warfare, and although I have more to learn, I am able to effectively assert apostolic authority over the enemy.

Since I know what to expect, the level of warfare that I experience is diminished. I know how to

- Assert my authority
- Overthrow principalities and powers
- Reign and rule from heavenly places
- Release judgement and attacks back onto the head of the enemy
- Remain positioned in the offense where I am above and ahead of the enemy
- How to use scripture the sword of the spirit against the enemy
- How to be assertive and offensive to discern and dismantle warfare before it attacks, and countless other tools of weaponry

Since I have embraced the mantle as my own I have taken the full responsibility of it so when I am attacked and experience warfare I am quick to pray and begin to search and seek God out for what it is so that I can pray strategically. I take the time to personally combat the warfare privately, and I have spent countless hours with my spiritual mother praying, and being trained to war through who I am as an apostle. Because of this the realms know me and they respond to me. Heaven knows me, earth and my spheres of influence know me, and hell knows me. As I continue to grow in the apostolic authority, power, and rank that is on my life, my influence will only increase and get stronger. My spiritual mother makes herself readily available to me, so no matter what it is and how late it is I know that I can call her at anytime and she will go to war with me and for me. She helps me to identify oppression and warfare, and provides wisdom on dwelling deeper into prayer and the word to root out attacks. And as she does this, it teaches me how to go deeper as I search out, identify and root out the attacks in my private time.

When my spiritual mother prays and goes to war, she is strategic like a surgeon. Praying with her, has groomed me to pray strategically like a surgeon as well. I have been taught to go into the enemies camp, and look beyond the surface, into the hiding places of the enemy with the light of God. We pray until there is full breakthrough and release of the attacks where nothing is left lingering.

I have also been built up in perseverance, long suffering, and endurance. When I experience attacks I have a wealth of knowledge and weaponry stored up in my arsenal that I know how to strategically use, and what weapons combat what. I am constantly learning and studying the enemy, and since I have taken personal responsibility for my calling, God is able to give me personal revelation that helps me advance.

My spiritual mother has also shaped and molded me where I am mentally and emotionally equipped to handle attacks. In knowing that warfare is a part of the lifestyle of an apostle, I can fortify myself where it does not wound me mentally and emotionally, cause hinderances in my everyday endeavors, or in towering over the warfare. She covers my inner man and helps to guard and protect my mental, emotional, and inner state, such that the warfare does not inflict wounds upon me that produce unhealthiness in my heart, soul, and identity. She teaches me how to not only engage successfully in the warfare, but how important it is to take care of my whole man, and how to heal and cleanse myself from the warfare.

Through the years I have learned a lot concerning warfare through mentoring and training, personal experience, and also through being an armorbearer. Upon God revealing who my spiritual mother was in my life, and I began to walk in ministry with her, he revealed to us that I was her armorbearer. As an armorbearer you hold the armor and are the shield in the war of another person. It also places you directly onto the frontline of the battlefield. The Holy Spirit taught me how to be an armorbearer. I seemed to be a natural at it as he would train me how to serve naturally and to spiritually cover my spiritual mother in ministry. Although I was a devoted soldier ready to serve I had no idea what being an armorbearer meant, I just had to walk it out. And as I walked it out Holy Spirit taught how to be victorious in battle.

I was on the frontlines of warfare concerning my spiritual mother and the work God would grant to our hands. I gained hands on training through seeing firsthand the attacks against her. And not just seeing them, but being called as one to pray, intercede, cover, take some hits for her, and thwart attacks before they came. So armorbearing was like warfare 101, 102, 103 and etc for me! I sense that one of the reasons amongst many that God strategically positioned me as an armorbearer was so that I could learn warfare hands on, and so that I would learn quickly by being thrusted into a realm of the calling that I truly had no knowledge about. All while walking very close to my spiritual mother, and even though I was covering her, she too was still a covering and a teacher for me. As I think about this, I am sure that made the devil mad because we were never uncovered. We covered one another, and I learn from her as I serve her.

As an armorbearer, I was in the trenches of the warfare. I did what the Lord told me to. I would

- Pray and intercede for my spiritual mother on my own time
- War against the spirits that were on assignment against her
- Command backlash attacks to dry up and die, thwarting attacks of front lash
- Pray for her health, her sleep, ministry assignments, etc.,

Holy Spirit used this as training to mature me as a warrior and as a weapon of destruction against the enemy and wickedness. I was not only an eye-witness to the attacks that rose against the apostolic calling, but a annihilator of the darkness.

In warring on behalf of the life of another, I was interceding as if it was my own life. This has taught me compassion and to esteem others as I would myself. So just as I pray for myself, I am sharp, keen, quick, and skilled in being able to pray for others. Apostles need those who can train, equip, and prepare them for the warfare they will be presented with. They also need the hands on training so they can be chiseled into skilled, keen, and sharp warriors who displace, conquering, towering over, and extinguish darkness.

THE WAR LIFE OF AN APOSTLE

Apostles will be:
- A spectator for men
- Constantly persecuted
- Subjected to imprisonment
- Suffer seasons of betrayal, slander, accusations, offense, & jealousy from people
- Endures & combats dishonor, whispering spirits, slander, & illegal reproach from demons & people
- Combats trafficking & hustling spirits who try to dishonor, abuse & use the apostle's gifts & the gifts of others for personal again
- Combats religious spirits, people & strongholds who are resistant to change & liberty in the Holy Spirit
- Combats carnality, false doctrine, demonic truths, perversion (the twisted thing) & idolatry
- Endures seasons of misunderstanding & persecution from family members; especially those who operate in generational strongholds, familiar spirits, habits, & curses
- Endure challenges with insecure people who are intimidated & inferior around confident people
- Will be deserted & abandoned; endures seasons of loneliness, isolation, & long suffering
- Persecuted for righteousness sake
- Constant warfare/lifestyle of warfare
- Suffer afflictions and infirmities
- Combats mind binding/blinding spirits, depression & weariness
- May experience a thorn in the flesh due to revelation & mighty exploits to keep the apostle humbled & submitted to Jesus
- Combat witches & warlocks

- Combat principalities & powers & spiritual wickedness in high places, demonic structures & kingdoms, & territorial spirits & entrapments
- Combat & demolishes demonic & man made walls, fortifications, & hindrances erected to stop or delay the apostolic work
- Combats demonic assignments, demonic & human wicked plots, time released curses, trials & tribulations
- Combats sieges, entrapments, & incantations, from demons, witches & warlocks, & people sent to bring trouble on every side
- Combats sexual & vile thoughts, traps, & defilement sent to contaminate the apostle's purity & holiness
- Combats continual negative thoughts & accusations sent to boggle the mind, instill fear, inadequacy & destroy confidence
- Tracked by demonic agents, watcher & squatter spirits sent to obtain information & report back to demonic camps & wicked people
- Combat demonic visitation, demonic dreams, dream manipulators, agents & importers when sleep
- Combat spirit realm attacks during sleep or when being translated in the spirit for kingdom work

Spend time familiarizing yourself with these levels of warfare and embracing them as a part of your calling. The more you enmesh with truth, the quicker it will be for you to live offensively, while asserting authority over the enemy and wickedness.

WARFARE AGAINST IDOLATRY

Apostles are holy principalities who battle idolatry, witchcraft, worldliness, wickedness, witches and warlocks.

Apostle Jackie Green states the following in her book, "*Spurned Into Apostleship:*"

Principalities respect principalities. Apostles are like "holy principalities" in the Spirit realm and they are sent by God to contend with evil principalities, power structures and people. While praying and meditating upon ranks and order, the Lord said to me that "apostles are like good principalities" themselves and are sent and set to stand up against evil principalities. A principality is a prince, a sphere, a territory who is sent by a King or Queen. An apostle is perceived by demonic principalities and powers in a region as a holy principality from the Lord. Apostles go into a region and with God's strategies are able to train an army and pull down demonic structures and then build up the Kingdom of God.

Being a holy principality is part of an apostle's ministry. As we govern in the manner, we assert authority over principalities and powers, while protecting people from getting hurt, backsliding, and being led astray by false doctrine. We also protects the church from being mixed with idolatry and witchcraft, such that they are able to walk and operate in pure relationship with the Lord. In addition, people are taught what really is of God and what is not of him, and then are able to go out into the world and be pure lights for God and his kingdom.

The warfare against these idolatry, principalities, and powers is extreme and constant. It will also be extreme warfare that the average believer will not experience or understand. Some of this combating will be conducted in the natural realm, while other wars will be conducted through the dream and vision realm, in heavenly realms, and through warfare and intercessory prayers. Apostles have authority in realms that most have never saw or experienced. Apostles have to be at peace that some of their experiences will appear fascinating, unbelievable and sometimes confusing to the average saint. Apostles will have to use wisdom regarding what to share and when to share as not to cause reproach or challenges upon the secret mysteries of their calling and the kingdom. Also where people will not idolize or become *"spooky spiritual"* regarding the mysteries of the kingdom, such that they fall into idolatry and sorcery when pursuing mysteries rather than God and allowing him to reveal and lead them into the mysteries of the kingdom.

Matthew 13:11 He answered and said unto them, Because it is given unto you to know the mysteries of the kingdom of heaven, but to them it is not given.

Mark 4:11 And he said unto them, Unto you it is given to know the mystery of the kingdom of God: but unto them that are without, all these things are done in parables.

<u>Mysteries is mystērion in the Greek and means:</u>

1. (to shut the mouth); a secret or "mystery" (through the idea of silence imposed by initiation into religious rites): — mystery

2. hidden thing, secret, mystery generally mysteries, religious secrets, confided only to the initiated and not to ordinary mortals
3. a hidden or secret thing, not obvious to the understanding
4. a hidden purpose or counsel secret will of men, of God
5. the secret counsels which govern God in dealing with the righteous, which are hidden from ungodly and wicked men but plain to the godly
6. in rabbinic writings, it denotes the mystic or hidden sense
    a. of an OT saying
    b. of an image or form seen in a vision
    c. of a dream

Example of Natural Warfare Against Idolatry & Principalities & Witchcraft: **Acts 16:16-18** *And it came to pass, as we went to prayer, a certain damsel possessed with a spirit of divination met us, which brought her masters much gain by soothsaying: The same followed Paul and us, and cried, saying, These men are the servants of the most high God, which shew unto us the way of salvation. And this did she many days. But Paul, being grieved, turned and said to the spirit, I command thee in the name of Jesus Christ to come out of her. And he came out the same hour.*

Example of Spiritual Warfare Against Idolatry & Principalities & Witchcraft: **Ephesians 6:12** *For we wrestle not against flesh and blood, but against principalities, against powers, against the rulers of the* darkness of this world, against spiritual wickedness in high places.

<u>High places</u> in the Greek is *epouranios* and means:

1. above the sky: — celestial, (in) heaven(-ly), high
2. existing in heaven things that take place in heaven
3. the heavenly regions heaven itself, the abode of God and angels the lower heavens, of the stars the heavens, of the clouds
4. the heavenly temple or sanctuary
5. of heavenly origin or nature

Principalities and powers are engaged in spiritual and natural realms. Spiritual wickedness in high places refers to spiritual realms – warfare that is taking place in the heavenly regions, heavenly sanctuaries and temples – above the skies. These are wicked plots, plans, assignments, sins, iniquities, and malice, being orchestrated and released by demonic kingdoms, wicked people, and witches and warlocks. This demonic debauchery is invisible to the natural realm seeming it is conducted in and through heavenly realms. These realms and entities were created to give God glory, but ended up being used by the enemies of God.

> ***Colossians 1:16*** *For by him were all things created, that are in heaven, and that are in earth, visible and invisible, whether they be thrones, or dominions, or principalities, or powers: all things were created by him, and for him.*

High ranking demons, witches and warlocks navigate through these realms because they understand their authority and jurisdiction. Apostles also have authority and jurisdiction in these realms. They will be lead by the Holy Spirit to fight and demolish these plans and assignments in heavenly realms, such that they are not released in the earth. As ambassadors of Christ, everything we do is from and through this perspective. We are seeking to do what Jesus does, even as Jesus only did what the father did (*John 5:19*).

Jesus fought all types of high ranking devils, wickedness, and powers in the natural realm, but he also overpowered principalities, powers and spiritual wickedness in high places within spiritual realms. These works are mentioned in the Bible, but not fully elaborated on. They are mysteries of the kingdom given to the mature believer –particularly the apostle - to complete and have revelation of, but not to those who cannot sufficiently govern in these realms.

> ***Psalms 68:18*** *Thou hast ascended on high, thou hast led captivity captive: thou hast received gifts for men; yea, for the rebellious also, that the LORD God might dwell among them.*
>
> ***Ephesians 4:8-10*** *Wherefore he saith, When he ascended up on high, he led captivity captive, and gave gifts unto men. (Now that he ascended, what is it but that he also descended first into the lower parts of the earth? He that descended is the same also that ascended up far above all heavens, that he might fill all things.)*
>
> ***Colossians 2:15*** *And having spoiled principalities and powers, he made a shew of them openly, triumphing over them in it.*

Apostles must understand that even as there are spiritual realms, dreams and visions are real realms. Science contends that we encounter five stages of rest before we actually enter deep sleep. Though science is unsure of the reason for the stages, they contend that throughout the night we can go in and out of these stages. As we enter a place of rest, our physical body goes to sleep and enters a stage of paralysis. Our brain is still active and is sending signals to our body to ensure we retain the necessary functions to maintain life as we sleep. Stage five is where we encounter REM (rapid eye movement) sleep aka as deep sleep. Though we can have visions and dreams in other stages, the REM stage is where most dreams occur and is where our heart rate increases, as it is pumping blood to our brain and other body parts to maintain life.

We learn from the bible that God who is all spirit (*Psalms 121:3-4*), never sleeps or slumbers, so our spirit never sleeps or slumbers. Though our flesh is asleep, our spirit man is active and open to receiving and working for God. God communicates with us via dreams and visions, while we are sleep or awake. He gives us revelations, strategies, direction, answers, warnings, prophetic insight, and assignments through dreams and visions. Sometimes we may think we are dreaming, but our spirit man is actually translated into realms in the spirit and/or the natural to do a work for God. We may heal the sick, release a word to people, ministries, or governments, combat principalities, powers, wickedness in high places, etc. Demons, witches, and warlocks use these realms to wage war against us. Because we do not adequately govern these realms, we end up with all kinds of demonic infiltration, infestations, impartations, depressions, and oppressions that could be avoided if we learn to navigate, maneuver, and operate in these areas of our calling. We must embrace these realms as doing so diminishes the warfare of the enemy taking advantage of our ignorance or our fear of governing over these realms as ambassadors of Christ.

OPERATING IN DREAM & SPIRITUAL REALMS

This chapter will provide nuggets for operating in dream and spiritual realms.

- Ask the Holy Spirit to begin teaching you about the spiritual realms to which you govern. Ask him to teach you about the principalities and powers, wickedness, witches and warlocks, you will be combating, and to give you weapons, insights, and strategies on how to annihilate them.
- Armor yourself in the weapons on *Ephesians 6*, while also asking God for specific weapons you can use during combat in the spirit realm and your dream and vision realms
- When combating such powers in the spiritual realm as you pray and intercede, use your weapons, angelic assistance, host of heaven, the word of God, and your authority to assert control over powers to defeat the enemy. Ask the Holy Spirit to fight with you, guide you in your military service, and trust him to lead you in asserting authority over the victory you have already obtained through the death and resurrection of Jesus Christ.
- Embrace your dreams and visions as a part of your calling, even the scary dreams and visions. They reveal military intel about the demonic kingdom, wickedness, and about the future challenges and destructions of the world.

- Spend time cleansing yourself of fear, anxiety related to interacting in your dreams and spiritual realms.
- Before going to sleep, command your spirit to be active and interactive in your dreams and visions. Declare that as you dream, you will be fully aware of what is occurring and will be so keen in your dreams, such that you will discern whether:
    - You are dreaming or that you are translated into a heavenly realm
    - Encountering familiar spirits and shape-shifters, demonic agents, principalities, powers, witches, warlocks, demonic manipulators and infiltrators, etc. and aware of your weapons and authority in defeating them
- If you find yourself running or being chased in your dreams, command your spirit to take authority in the dream, to stop running, and to counter attack whatever is attacking you.
- Remember fear is not your portion. Because dreams occur in real realms, you have the power to assert authority over dreams and change them. Depending on what is going on in a dream, I will call for angelic assistance, chase whatever was chasing me, and beat down whatever attacking me. I may also command myself to wake up, especially if I feel I am unsafe in a dream or if I am striving to attack in my natural strength rather than from the spiritual strength of my calling and mantle. I then cleanse myself of all fear, anxiety, and any traumatic events or tragedy the enemy is trying to instill in my life through the dream. I then

will ask God to send angels to deal with what occurred in the dream, while decreeing judgment against whatever was attacking me in my dream.

COMBATING TERRITORIAL WARFARE & WITCHCRAFT

A skilled warrior learns about and studies their opponent. The warrior is studying his opponent not because of fear but to be offensive in warfare. Also the more the warrior knows and can discern regarding demonic forces, the easier it is to resist and combat them in one's personal life and ministry.

Many would say this is not biblical, but much of the Old Testament stories of war reveal key principles to successfully learning and annihilating the enemy. Though we are no longer fight to obtain, but from a position of governing over our victory, we must not be ignorant of the devices of demons and wickedness.

> *1Peter 5:8 Be sober, be vigilant; because your adversary the devil, as a roaring lion, walketh about, seeking whom he may devour:*

Sober means to be *"self-controlled, prudent, wise, temperate, governed, and alert."*

Vigilant means to *"take watch, watch keenly to detect danger, be cautious, take heed, give strict attention to."*

Both of these attributes require action, strategy, and discipline.

- Your life has to be postured in the appropriate character of God
- You have to be disciplined in your character and faith stance

- You also have to be keen in being able to identify, resist, and destroy the devil as he attacks

Now the devil is roaming, treading, and seeking. He is on the prowl – on the hunt. He is doing the work to learn you. You must therefore do the work vigilantly to learn him. When you take watch you are on guard. You have already spied out the land and the enemy so you can implement strategy to best identify the enemy should he come, and to guard and protect everything from being overtaken when he attacks. It is not a passive position, but an aggressive, active duty of combat.

As the warrior studies their opponent, they are learning the following:

- Their character, nature, and personality
- Abilities and capabilities
- Likes and dislikes
- Habits and patterns
- Strengths and weaknesses
- Movements and operations
- Environments and habitats to which they maneuver and dwell
- Their identity, purpose, and mission
- Their personal, geographical, and generational power and operation
- History, culture, language and communication strategies

In studying your opponent, the warring apostle is conducting a spiritual mapping of the people, climate, government, and territory to which they live and are called to. I also suggest conducting a spiritual mapping over regions to which you are called to minister in. When completing a spiritual mapping, you are

- Seeking Holy Spirit for knowledge of the main principles, powers, idolatries, witchcraft, worldliness, and perversions that reign in that region.
- You can also drive around the region and receive this information via Holy Spirit
- Acquire information from online geographical and history studies of the region.

This information needs to be typed out and prayed into and used as the Holy Spirit leads. I suggest providing a copy to your prayer and support team, so they can use it when warring and interceding for you, the ministry and region in general.

At KSM, we have placed the principalities and strongholds that God revealed to us concerning our region in our ministry's new members handbook. We deem it important for people to know what they are dealing with. Many tend to leave a region they are called to before it is time, because they dread the warfare. If they were provided revelation of what to expect from the demonic realm and how to combat it, they are more apt to embrace their assignment with confidence and peace in knowing they can successfully completing the work God has granted to their hands.

Spiritual mapping allows the apostolic warrior to be offensive in fortifying themselves against the assignments of the enemy. It is also effective in the Holy Spirit leading the apostle in what strongholds and forces to deal with for that particular prayer assignment. It is not wise to take on every principality and power. Apostles are more effective in warfare when they operate as the spirit leads. Sometimes, displacing or annihilating certain strongholds can dismantle other ones by default. Being spirit lead will prevent unnecessary warfare and labor.

It is important to note that witches and warlocks pray against ministries and leaders within their territory. They pursue information of who the gatekeepers are and they spend countless hours sending spells, curses, and demonic assignments hinder, stifle, and kill the word of the Lord.

Sometimes they physically visit and release curses and incantations on the people, land, atmosphere, assignments of leaders and the ministries. In addition they will astral project into homes, ministries and regions to release curses, spells, and demonic assignments. They will even physically war, seek to intimidate, and afflict leaders, ministries, and visions as they project themselves through spiritual portals.

Witches tend to operate during the witching hours of 12am to 3am. They, however will do their work all day and night for the purposes and inciting evil upon God's people and kingdom. They are committed to their assignments. We too must be fervent in our offense in canceling these attacks before they are released.

With the rising use of social media and the online web, witches and warlocks spiritually map and track leaders and ministries through these means. They utilize the information as manipulators to release curses, spells, and demonic assignments. We must be careful what we release online. We must also be cognizant that the web has its own set of realms and influences. It is a global sphere. We must close off and thwart the attacks and assignments that are being unleashed through these portals and gateways.

I tend to declare that witchcraft works boomerang back upon the senders' own lives, families, and camps. There are instances I will send it back seven times stronger, or destroy it and their kingdom all together. Holy Spirit will lead you with how to combat these attacks. The key is to deal with them. They are the main reason many visions do not come to pass, never reach full maturity, or experience the level of fruit God intended for their lives and ministries. I decree we are SHIFTING as apostolic warriors in being sober and vigilant soldiers that dismantle and devour the works of the enemy. **SHIFT!**

DEMONIC SPIRITS & WITCHCRAFT THAT ATTACK APOSTLES

If you or the ministry is experiencing the following attacks, it is possible that you are dealing with spirits and witchcraft assignments sent through territorial warfare.

- <u>**Zapping Spirit**</u> – Bombards, jolts, snatches, strikes, deletes, steals, kills, revelation, thoughts, and understanding from the mind, such that the brain cannot send the correct signals to the body.

    John 10:10 *The thief cometh not, but for to steal, and to kill, and to destroy: I am come that they might have life, and that they might have it more abundantly.*

- <u>**Blocking Spirits**</u> - Use walls, barriers or troops of demons that have locked themselves together in the spirit realm, where a you will have difficulty getting pass a particular barrier. This will feel like a wall, gate, ceiling, door, object hindering breakthrough or a pathway from opening. You may also feel this in your mind and heart where you cannot seem to SHIFT pass a certain thought, issue, or barrier that has lodged itself in these areas.

    Psalms 18:29 *For by thee I have run through a troop; and by my God have I leaped over a wall.*

This scriptures lets us know that we must run through these barriers. So when encountering them, verbally declare out blasting through any troops that have set up siege against you and then use your authority in God to leap over demonic structures.

- **_Python Spirits_** - Wrap around a person, family, situation, ministry, or region, while using its body to squeeze and restrict them where:
    o They are limited in mobility and progress
    o There may also be an unexplainable tiredness and lethargic oppression where energy, movement, and progress is slow or thwarted
    o There will be a weightiness, physical suffocation, over exerted in energy, and sluggardness to being in step with the momentum of of God
    o It causes confusion, discombobulation, double mindedness, and thought racing, from the signal faculties in the brain being restricted, weighty, and crushed

Isaiah 61:3 To appoint unto them that mourn in Zion, to give unto them beauty for ashes, the oil of joy for mourning, the garment of praise for the spirit of heaviness; that they might be called trees of righteousness, the planting of the Lord, that he might be glorified.

Break the head and tail of the python. Loose Holy fire to torment it where it releases its grip, while commanding this spirit to uncoil and be cast out of your midst.

- **_Spirit of Leviathan_** - Interrupts and distorts communication between the speaker and the listener, between God and the person/ministry, and within atmospheres. Its' effort is to sow offense, discord, irritation, anger, misunderstanding, faultfinding, ungodly judging, mistrust and suspicion. Job speaks of how Leviathan operates in *Job 41:26-32*. This spirit was in operation between him and his friends who were striving to understand why God allowed the enemy to bring havoc upon his life. This spirit also distorted Job's views where he could not receive wise counsel from God during this time of trial with the Lord. This spirit will enter in when the ministry is under heavy warfare, is in the middle of intense ministry or transition, or is on a time schedule with completing a ministry piece.

Quick repentance and forgiveness is the easiest way to combat against leviathan. The unity and love of Christ will dismantle and displace this spirit.

Galatians 6:1-3 The Amplified Bible BRETHREN, *IF any person is overtaken in misconduct or sin of any sort, you who are spiritual [who are responsive to and controlled by the Spirit] should set him right and restore and reinstate him, without any sense of superiority and with all gentleness, keeping an attentive eye on yourself, lest you should be tempted also. Bear (endure, carry) one another's burdens and troublesome moral faults, and in this way fulfill and observe perfectly the law of Christ (the Messiah) and complete what is lacking [in your obedience to it].*

Cut the head and the tail off of this spirit and release fire to burn up its fruits and roots, while casting it out of your sphere.

- *<u>Mind Binding & Mind Blinding Spirits</u>* – Witches love to operate through the stronghold of mind control. These spirits bind and blind the thought life, the mind and senses to cause affliction, confusion, unexplainable fear of people or of failure, and anxiety. Have trouble paying attention, experience mind wandering and racing thoughts. This spirit tends to operate and look like an octopus or a squid. You may feel pressure or a tormenting headache, feel like something is sticking you in the eyes, ears, temples, forehead, or the back of the head. Things may look black as you strain to see and discern spiritually and naturally. You may become dull of hearing because the ears will feel clogged or like something is lodged in them. It may also feel like something is sitting on your head or wrapped around your head.

This stronghold of mind control may also plague you with vile, perverse, unnecessary, or unimportant thoughts. Or may have you panicking and thinking of something over and over to distract you from what is presently important. Sometimes this spirit will swamp you with constant thoughts of hurts from your past or present life and heart issues that are unresolved. You may find it difficult to pay attention or to press forward in working on present tasks because of these constant plaguing thoughts and feelings of intense pressure.

Proverbs 15:15 The Amplified Bible *All the days of the desponding and afflicted are made evil [by anxious thoughts and forebodings (prophecy)], but he who has a* *glad heart has a continual feast [regardless of circumstances].*

Ask the Lord to sever the tentacles of this spirit or use the sword of the spirit to cut them. Break the power of pressure, pain and torment, and release healing where needed.

- **Spirit of Void & Darkness** - May be at work when there are no blockages, hinderances, blinding, binding, confusion or discombobulation, yet the atmosphere, eye gates, imagination and mind is totally black and blank, dark and empty. We see this spirit in operation in *Genesis 1:2* when God was creating the heavens and the earth.

And the earth was without form, and void; and darkness was upon the face of the deep. And the Spirit of God moved upon the face of the waters

This spirit wants you to think that everything is dead and without form, you cannot see or discern properly, or that there is no potential for creation or manifestation. It operates like a black blanket or cloud, covering everything so you cannot see behind the scenes. It will smother blackness and void over the plans and seeds of God, and even conceal demonic plans so you cannot be offensive against the enemy. It will black out the ability to vision, receive revelation, purpose for ministry engagements, and plots and plans of the enemy.

Daniel 2:22 *He reveals the deep and secret things; He knows what is in the darkness, and the light dwells with Him.*

When this spirit attacks begin to release and declare the light, wisdom, and profound, searchable, secretive, mysteries of God to come forth to dispel the darkness.

- **_Spirits of Fear_** – Different types of fear can be sent through witchcraft and territorial attacks. Fear is a distressing emotion, concern or anxiety aroused by impending danger, evil, pain, sweating, rejection, etc., whether the threat is real or imagined. It is the feeling or condition of being afraid, frightened, panicked, anxious disheveled, frenzied, overwhelmed, gripped, shocked or traumatized with terror. Fear can be sent as a spell or assignment through the atmosphere, imparted into the mind or imagination through mind manipulation, bewitchment, or telepathy; imparted via dreams, or by through demonic creativity or stirring via witchcraft of a traumatic or startling event to incite fear. Fear tends to attack unaware; it can have no real basis for manifesting, but its presence if very real, intentional, and demonic.

2Timothy 1:7 For God hath not given us the spirit of fear; but of power, and of love, and of a sound mind.

When we yield to fear, we SHIFT from under the authority, love, and stability of God. We believe the lies, misperceptions, misconceptions of the enemy, while, relenting to instability, weakness, and helplessness. We also resort to believing we are worthless, under appreciated, devalued, and that our life is not worth living. The more you meditate and yield to the thoughts, the greater the fear and the oppression of its assignment. Fear is an attack and assignment against the truth of your identity and against your salvation and refuge in God.

Bind and cast out the spirit of fear. Break the powers of how it is manifesting, fall out of agreement with any ways you agreed with fear, close up portals to it operating again, use scriptures to build your identity and fortify yourself in the love and worth of God.

- **_Spirit of Confusion_** – Causes chaos, disorder, upheaval, forgetfulness, cloudiness, frustration, blankness, and discombobulation. May be unable to distinguish right from wrong, truth from lies, clearness from distinctiveness. Such attacks causes uncertainty of self and others, uncertainty of one's calling, confusion of one's destiny vision; will cause you to question your identity, your team, supports, and God. You will begin to waver as the chaos causes a tossing to and fro between reality and delusion.

1Corinthians 14:33 For God is not the author of confusion, but of peace, as in all churches of the saints.

Break the powers and spells of confusion and bewitchment. Cleanse out all effects of how the spirit is operating in your life, atmosphere and ministry.

- **_Spirit of the Sluggardness_** – The spirit of the sluggardness is sent to cause inactivity, idleness, laziness, relaxed, dull, and disinterested. There may be an exhaustion where you are sleeping for long periods of time or for no apparent reason, not wanting to be bothered, or wanting to hide from people and responsibilities. You can be indolent, slow moving, sluggish, averse or disinclined to work, be active, or to exert energy. This spirit will cause you to lack wisdom, vision, and energy in knowing when to plant, work, and invest. It feels like a weight laying upon you. It can sometimes feel cold clammy, wet, moist, or slimy where you feel uncomfortable or unclean. You have an intent and heart to work, but no drive.

Matthew 26:41 Watch and pray, that ye enter not into temptation: the spirit indeed is willing, but the flesh is weak.

Proverbs 6:6-9 Go to the ant, thou sluggard; consider her ways, and be wise: Which having no guide, overseer, or ruler, Provideth her meat in the summer, and gathereth her food in the harvest. How long wilt thou sleep, O sluggard? when wilt thou arise out of thy sleep?

Bind and cast out the spirit of the sluggard. Break its power off your physical body, health, mind, and heart. You may also have to break its power off the body, health, mind heart of your ministry, region and people you oversee. Cleanse your foundation, life and ministry of any patterns of sluggardness, laziness, making excuses, and inconsistency.

- *Spirit of Slander & Accusation* – Releasing fiery darts, word curses, accusations, gossip, ungodly reports, malice, and defamation against one's character, ministry, or work. The slander is generally false or the true being used in a slanderous way to incite shame, shunning, condemnation, and destruction.

Sometimes you cannot resolve slander natural. When slander cannot be resolved, know that God judges the slanderous.

Matthew 12:36 But I tell you that every careless word that people speak, they shall give an accounting for it in the day of judgment.

Other times slander can be resolved through healthy conflict resolution skills and healthy communication. But the spirit of slander and accusation is still at work in your soul and in the spirit. It will need to be rebuked and its assignment will need to be cancelled. The true report of the Lord will need to be declared into your life and the spirit realm.

Proverbs 11:9 The Amplified Bible With his mouth the godless man destroys his neighbor, but through knowledge and superior discernment shall the righteous be delivered.

Proverbs 26:20-22 Where no wood is, there the fire goeth out: so where there is no talebearer, the strife ceaseth. As coals are to burning coals, and wood to fire; so is a contentious man to kindle strife. The words of a talebearer are as wounds, and they go down into the innermost parts of the belly.

- **Spirits of Affliction & Infirmities** – Sometimes apostles will endure constant or seasonal attacks in this area. Some attacks may be related to soul issues or a part of the generation lineage. God may send an affliction as a form of buffeting to keep the apostle humble and submitted to him. Other times afflictions and infirmities are sent by witches and territorial spirits to bind, distract, hinder, and attack the apostle. When words curses are released, they may come in the form of affliction. It is important for apostles to really pray over their food because the enemy and witches will inflict by casting spells upon meals and drinks.

Many times, we may go to the doctor and they are not able to cure or relieve us of ailments. When there are no open doors for the affliction and infirmities, then it is most likely due to territorial warfare or witchcraft. As an apostle, it is also possible to carry the afflictions of the people, ministry, land, and region you are governing. Often when I pray deliverance and healing prayers for myself I pray for these areas as well for when they are delivered and healed, I at times am relieved of afflictions and infirmities.

There are also instances where I will visit a region and become afflicted or infirmed. Generally, it is because my body is manifesting the ailments of that region, or the witches and territorial spirits of that region are attacking me because of the calling and mantle upon my life. The Holy Spirit can reveal to you how to counterattack this to judge and break whatever is binding you such that deliverance is your portion.

> ***Psalms 34:17-20*** *The righteous cry, and the Lord heareth and delivereth them out of all their troubles. The Lord is nigh unto them that are of a broken heart; and saveth such as be of a contrite spirit. Many are the afflictions of the righteous: but the Lord delivereth him out of them all. He keepeth all his bones: not one of them is broken.*

God has promised to deliver the righteous from every affliction. This is so key to remaining in a posture of peace and confidence that he will deliver, especially when the affliction and infirmity releases feelings and reports of helplessness, no cure or death. Apostles constantly face death, but God delivers them out of attack for his glory.

> ***1Corinthians 4:9*** *For I think that God hath set forth us the apostles last, as it were appointed to death: for we are made a spectacle unto the world, and to angels, and to men.*

- **_Spirit of Jezebel_** – Jezebel tends to manifest everywhere(e.g. on the job, at church, in the service, in the boardroom, at the grocery story, at the family event, online, in your email). I believe this spirit tracks apostles and prophets. It also shape shifts from person to person, where it manifests in different situations in the prophet's and the apostle's life. Though some people you encounter will have the Jezebel spirit, this spirit also oppresses insecure people or people who have a need to be validated. It uses them to frustrate, control, intimidate, and challenge the mantle and work of the apostle. Jezebel will seduce, manipulate people and situations to stir up strife against the apostle and the work of the apostle. Jezebel will gain personal knowledge on the apostle, particularly about their past, then use it to launch witchcraft drama and conflict against the apostle and the vision of the ministry. This spirit is so manipulative and webbing, that it will have you questioning yourself even though your motives of pure for the people and work at hand, you are delivered from that sin, and you have not done another wrong.

Jezebel must be confronted naturally and spiritually. Its' actions must be exposed in both realms such that the influences and works are totally annihilated off the people, ministry, region, and in regards to any seeds and fruits it may have planted within the word of people, ministries, and the region. When confronted Jezebel will be defensive, prideful, and will seek to gain the approval and strength of the naysayers to prove that her actions are Godly and for the good of the people and the ministry. Jezebel is intelligent, skilled, and knows how to articulate where its' plot sounds like the true will of the Lord. The situation will most likely get messy and very confrontational, even unto death (spiritually and or naturally), before it gets better. Jezebel however, will not submit to leadership or the vision of the ministry, as it usurps authority. As this is exposed, people will discern its true intent, such that its plans revealed and thwarted.

Jezebel will come at the apostle very abrupt, matter of fact, and strong. This is because of the demons operating behind the scenes to strengthen her assignment, and the witchcraft that has been sent to fortify its work against the apostle and the work of the ministry. Jezebel is not stronger than the Lord, and is not stronger that the apostle's or prophet's mantle. Do not allow Jezebel to cower you. Stand up to this spirit, deal with it naturally and in prayer, the watch God get glory through every situation.

2Kings 9:9-11 The Amplified Bible *I will make the house of Ahab like the house of Jeroboam son of Nebat and like the house of Baasha son of Ahijah. And the dogs shall eat Jezebel in the portion of Jezreel, and none shall bury her. And he opened the door and fled. [Fulfilled in II Kings 9:33-37.]*

Micah 5:12 *And I will cut off witchcrafts out of thine hand; and thou shalt have no [more] soothsayers:*

Revelation 2:20 *Notwithstanding I have a few things against thee, because thou sufferest that woman Jezebel, which calleth herself a prophetess, to teach and to seduce my servants to commit fornication, and to eat things sacrificed unto idols.*

- <u>***Spirit of Goliath***</u> – Goliath seeks to defy the name, plans, and work of the Lord. Goliath will challenge the apostle and use intimidating tactics to get the apostle to back down from fulfilling the vision at hand. Witches and territorial spirits will send constant intimidating thoughts to the apostle through the well of Goliath. The thoughts are so intense, piercing, and continuous that the apostle will start to feel overwhelmed, burdened, inadequate, angry, and want to give up, hide, or separate themselves from people and the vision. The apostle will not want to war against Goliath for fear that they will be defeated. There will also be natural confrontations within the apostle's life that will strengthen and confirm the attacks being sent in the spirit realm. These attacks may come through family members, bosses, etc. It is usually through people who have a level of authority and influence and is being used to cower, isolate, and cause a withdrawing of the apostle from walking in their mantle and from the vision.

Sometimes the witchcraft attacks coming through Goliath can cause pain, such as migraines, stomach aches, panic attacks or chest pains. An unwarranted fear or intimidated presence maybe accompanied with these attacks. Goliath is a big in stature, and boastful in puffed up chatter, but the apostle is greater, and so is the authority of God in the apostle's life. Do not go back and forth in mindless and puffed up words with Goliath. Apostles know who they, are so they have nothing to prove to Goliath or anyone else. Use your weapons and authorities to smite him in the forehead. Explore the heart of situations concerning Goliath, then use the word of God to stab him in the heart with the sword of God's word and plans for your life and the vision at hand, then cut off his head to totally solidify his defeat against you and God's vision.

1Samuel 17:48-51 The Amplified Bible When the Philistine came forward to meet David, David ran quickly toward the battle line to meet the Philistine. David put his hand into his bag and took out a stone and slung it, and it struck the Philistine, sinking into his forehead, and he fell on his face to the earth.

So David prevailed over the Philistine with a sling and with a stone, and struck down the Philistine and slew him. But no sword was in David's hand. So he ran and stood over the Philistine, took his sword and drew it out of its sheath, and killed him, and cut off his head with it. When the Philistines saw that their mighty champion was dead, they fled.

- **<u>Spirit of Death & Hell</u>** – Can attack the person, families, ministries, and the region. There will be a dark presence and experience of doom and gloom, extreme heaviness upon the atmosphere, over your life, in your heart and chest. There will be flooding thoughts of dying and killing yourself, wanting to die and be with Jesus even though it is not time to leave the earth. There will be constant near death experiences, fears of tragedies, demonic dreams to instill fear of dying; attacks spiritually and physically through the spirit of murder, sabotage, and self-sabotage.

  Cancel witchcraft spells and assignments, rebuke spirits of death – send them back to hell if necessary. Cleanse out dream impartations of fear and tragedy and cancel assignments sent through dreams. Agree and decree out life and that more abundantly. Remember as an apostle, you have resurrection power. Use it to combat death and hell.

John 10:10 *The thief cometh not, but for to steal, and to kill, and to destroy: I am come that they might have life, and that they might have it more abundantly.*

Apostles must be fervent in praying against witchcraft and territorial warfare. Both my spiritual mothers are prayer warriors and instilled within me the importance of fervency. My spiritual mother, Apostle Kathy Williams taught me endurance in prayer. We would spend hours, even days praying on a matter. We would have personal prayer shut ins, where we would close in for days and just pray. She is a praiser, worshipper, and overcomer. She has an unprecedented ability to endure hardship as a good soldier and to outlast the trial of any devil or challenging situation. She has taught me how to love, reverence, and trust God no matter what is occurring in my life, and to persevere through the agonies of life and warfare. She has also taught me loyalty to God, his vision, and loved ones. Even if she did not know how to stop my warfare, the purpose of it, or how to help me through it, she has been loyal and diligent in praying for me, supporting me, and enduring with me. She has spent countless hours and days interceding for me, protecting, nurturing, and covering me in the spirit. She has a mothering heart for me as a biological mother does for her child, so she shelters me in the spirit as if she physically birthed me herself. This has taught me how to pray through even when I have to do so through blind faith, and that loyalty, diligence and love will conquer any demonic force attempting to thwart my destiny and the destiny of those I govern.

My spiritual mother Apostle Jackie Green is a skilled warrior of prayer. Like me, God reveals attacks and spirits to her, and gives her strategic prayers, decrees, and prophecies to annihilate the enemy. She has written multiple books on prayer, deliverance, and warfare. I am able to glean from these works to combat the enemy.

> ***James 5:16*** *Confess your faults one to another, and pray one for another, that ye may be healed. The effectual fervent prayer of a righteous man availeth much.*

I decree that you would always have a desire to pray, a love to pray, a fervency to pray and that perseverance in prayer and warfare is infused into your mantle and calling. I decree every demon that combats you will be quickly exposed, that you take joy in knowing that you prevail over every demon, and that the end result is that you are victorious. May you SHIFT with increasing in your identity and authority even now. May you SHIFT in towering all the more in wearing the truth of your mantle, experiencing God, and him receiving limitless glory out of your life. **SHIFT!**

WARFARE DUE TO DIVINE VISIONS & REVELATIONS

2Corinthians 12:1-7 It is not expedient for me doubtless to glory. I will come to visions and revelations of the Lord. I knew a man in Christ above fourteen years ago, (whether in the body, I cannot tell; or whether out of the body, I cannot tell: God knoweth;) such an one caught up to the third heaven. And I knew such a man, (whether in the body, or out of the body, I cannot tell: God knoweth;) How that he was caught up into paradise, and heard unspeakable words, which it is not lawful for a man to utter. Of such an one will I glory: yet of myself I will not glory, but in mine infirmities. For though I would desire to glory, I shall not be a fool; for I will say the truth: but now I forbear, lest any man should think of me above that which he seeth me to be, or that he heareth of me. And lest I should be exalted above measure through the abundance of the revelations, there was given to me a thorn in the flesh, the messenger of Satan to buffet me, lest I should be exalted above measure.

<u>Revelations</u> in this passage of scripture is *apokalypsis* and means:

1. disclosure, appearing, coming, lighten, manifestation, be revealed, revelation, appearance
2. laying bare, making naked, a disclosure of truth
3. instruction concerning things before unknown used of events by which things or states or persons hitherto withdrawn from view are made visible to all

Many claim to be buffeted with afflictions and situations, but do not realize that if this is the case, there must be potential for a character discrepancy that God is striving to keep them from exhibiting. They also do not realize that this buffeting is ordained by God - designed by God to keep Paul humble where he would not exalt himself above God or steal God's glory. God is using demonic warfare to humble them and keep them submitted to him. Because it is ordained by God, it is not a warfare that can be prayed away. *Buffet* in the Greek means to *"strike with the fist, yield a blow."* So regardless to the enemy striking you with pain and adversity, your victory is not in striking him back. It is in the the sufficiency of grace that God gives. His grace is unfailing, and yields strength to conquer and remain fortified in the works of God, despite the constant buffeting of the enemy.

It is important to discern buffeting versus warfare from the demonic camp. Many are bound by warfare and contending it is God. Yet the signs and revelation of such warfare is not evident in their lives. And some are contending it is the devil combating them when it is God designed warfare sent to humble them in their walk unto him. This means that due to the mantle and calling on your life, there is a propensity in your character to steal glory and exalt yourself above God. I believe we should be learning from Paul's experience of buffeting rather than glorying in being like him. I have received multiple words that this is the reason I suffer great affliction. I however, strive to work on my character and posture of humility, rather than surrendering to demons striking me with blows. Apostles should possess a grand reverence for God where a buffeting is not needed in their lives. There should be a continual caution and checking of one's motives and character in effort to avoid needing to be buffeted in one's humility.

WARFARE WITH THE SOUL ISSUES
OF PEOPLE & MINISTRIES

Apostles will have to help ministries, mentees, and spiritual children who God has assigned to their lives. Yet at times, because of their soulish and heart issues, the enemy will have them believing the apostle is their enemy and do not have their best interest at heart. This will be challenging for the apostle and even hurtful at times. Especially since the apostle will still be required to pour their life out into the ministry and/or the person. The apostle will have to remain unoffended and not take little jabs and misunderstandings personal. This can be difficult at times as the apostle will have to pick his or her battles as to not be distracted where the ultimate vision is being hindered or impacted.

It is important for the apostle to take their hurts and offenses to the Lord so he or she can cleanse, heal, and provide clarity on whether to address these challenges or to remain focused on the vision at hand. Sometimes it will be necessary to address it, and sometime it will be best to remain focused on the work of the Lord. This is important because apostles cannot apologize for who they are and cannot continually be focused on making those who struggle with rejection, inferiority or insecurity feel comfortable. Apostles also cannot speed up their healing process, especially if they are not ready. The apostle must trust God to work in them as he or she continues to be who they need to be to their lives and to the ministry. This can be a challenge as at times such people can be open doors to the enemy attacking you as an apostle. They can be open doors to:

- Betrayal
- Denial of your calling and work
- Gossip, slander (cannot chase either)
- Planting seeds of negativity into others who are a part of the vision
- Speaking for you since they are close to you or are a part of the vision but cause division, suspicion, and misunderstanding, because they speak through familiarity and not through truth
- Hinderances to the vision as they resist doing their part, or are passive aggressive in completing their part of the vision as payback of challenges they have regarding your role in their lives and the ministry
- Taking jabs at you where they try to make you responsible for their lack of healing or progress, when really it is their own insecurity and rejection issues that hinder than process

Remember Jesus knew the apostles would deny him, betray him, make him prove he was the Messiah, strive to get him prove his dedication, and protection of them, etc., but he still had to:

- Personally mentor them
- Deem them friends and sons
- Declare them partners, affiliates, and successors of his ministry and kingdom
- Disciple, train, equip them
- Love and empower them

- Share the vision of ministry and the kingdom with them
- Complete ministry with them

I placed this revelation in the warfare section because there will be a constant combating of these type of challenges for the apostle.

- The apostle will be at war with remaining compassionate and focused on the vision at hand versus yielding to his or her flesh and soul, where they will want to snap on people, cut people off, and not want to be who God is requiring them to be to these ministries and people.
- The apostle will war in his her own ability and calling as an apostle, as such attacks will make them feel inadequate at times; and even search themselves as to whether the actions of people are due to them doing something wrong or not really hearing from God.
- The apostle will be constantly healing his or her own wounds before the Lord and guarding themselves in not allowing continual offenses and challenges to reopen wounds, as these people are processed with God in their healing, or as the vision of God unfolds in the ministries.
- The apostle will have to be patient and not allow negative thoughts from the enemy draw them into proving themselves or doing things in effort to gain the favor and trust of such people and ministries. Because they are operating from a wounded soul and heart issues, their issues will have to be constantly fed by such actions, which

can be tiring and stressful. The apostle has to understand that such people and ministries require a processing with God and no amount of proving will heal the wounds that only God can fulfill in the identity of such people and ministries.

Warfare Exploration Prayer & Activation

1. What apostolic warfare do you endure?
2. How have you embraced warfare to this point in your apostolic walk?
3. What are your thoughts and feelings regarding warfare being your career as an apostle?
4. How has the revelation in this book empowered you in your career in the military service of God's kingdom?
5. What needs to SHIFT in you to further embrace your warfare call and live from the position of being offensive as career apostolic warrior?
6. Spend time before God cleansing yourself of the wounds and pains that has come from past and present seasons of warfare. Forgive God and people as necessary and ask him to heal you where necessary (Make this a consistent part of your prayer life).
7. Ask God to give you a love and peace with embracing warfare.
8. Go forth in beating the devil down for God's glory! **SHIFT!**

COMBATING RELIGION & TRADITION
2Corinthians 3:17 Now the Lord is that Spirit: and where the Spirit of the Lord is, there is liberty.

Liberty in the Holy Spirit permits the freedom to omit things that have nothing to do with the salvation of Jesus Christ. Apostles exemplify the freedom of the Lord – the freedom of the Holy Spirit. Their freedom is demonstrated through everything that they do. This is because apostles live a life inside the Holy Spirit. They are full of the Holy Spirit, and instill the freedom of the Holy Spirit into people, ministries, atmospheres, and regions. Apostles birth and establish the liberation and momentum of God through the mantles and visions of God upon their lives.

Religion and tradition hates freedom. Religion and tradition deems freedom unstable, unbiblical, and flighty. Religion and tradition is rooted in doctrine and religious facts. It however, rejects the supernatural and any parts of God that it cannot control or understood through intellect and reasoning. Religion and tradition also steals and kills the presence, move, and momentum of God. It works through people, doctrines, and religious structures, to establish high places and monuments that claim to honor God, but really it stifles the will, abilities, power, fruit and progress of God.

Religion and tradition tends to be inflexible, intimidating, controlling, and will ostracize any one who refuse to operate within its barriers and boundaries. The mantle upon the apostle will not allow them to be restricted or to succumb to religious perimeters. Even if God allows the apostle to minister to religious and traditional people and ministries, they may naturally respect the structures that are set, but spiritually the mantle upon their lives will be contending and pushing out the structures and barriers. The apostle's very presence will impart the liberation of the Holy Spirit into the people, atmosphere, and region. A stirring for more of God will be ignited, and even cause friction for those who begin to pursue their new awakening in God.

The apostle must be aware of this as religious and traditional powers may confront them in the natural. They will also send retaliation and backlash in the spirit realm. The apostle must remain independent and liberated despite the attacks that will come through religion and tradition.

Apostles have to trust the impartations they instill into people and ministries.

> *1Corinthians 3:6 I have planted, Apollos watered; but God gave the increase.*

Sometimes apostles plant, other times they water. Apostles have to be okay that people will not always be able to handle or be ready to receive all that they desire to give or have to give. This will be a challenge at times, as apostles can see beyond where the people and the ministry is, and will want to SHIFT them to that place. However, people and ministries sometimes are not ready, or have a process to being liberated in the wealth and fullness of God.

Religion and tradition cause people and ministries to be closed minded related to their thinking and experiences concerning God. They tends to have relationship with God through their doctrine rather than their journey with him. They have to learn God from a liberated posture of his salvation, love, and grace. This is the reason Jesus spent most of his ministry teaching and equipping. He knew that even though people would witness him saving the world, most people, would still need to be processed out of religious and traditional clutches into relationship with him.

- Apostles must live in peace concerning their relationship with Jesus and be a comfortable with being a representative of a liberated walk with him.
- It is easy to build new high places and structures when SHIFTING out of religion and tradition. Apostles must help people and ministries avoid this, as the religious and traditional is familiar with the comfort of knowledge and control. They are not comfortable with completely trusting the presence, voice, foundational truths, and momentum of God.
- Apostles must teach people and ministries balance so that they have a solid biblical foundation that enables them to walk in the standards and principles of God, and though they are now liberated, not yield to witchcraft and idolatry in delving into areas of the supernatural that are illegal and ungodly.

Balance will deter the fixation upon the new experiences that will come from operating through the freedom of the Holy Spirit. People and ministries will have a love for solid biblical truth and for the Holy Spirit. They will understand that both are required in order to walk in a healthy relationship with Jesus. When either becomes a high place, they will have revelation that they have given back over to structures, witchcraft and idolatry.

EXPOSING SPIRITUAL TRAFFICKING

This topic is so essential because apostles must be careful not to be spiritually trafficked. They must also be protectors in others being subject to spiritual trafficking.

According to humantraffickinghotlineorg, human trafficking "*is modern-day slavery and involves the use of force, fraud, or coercion to obtain some type of labor or commercial sex act.*" The person is stolen from there family and region, and forced to live an enslaved life in an unfamiliar and impoverished environment.

Trafficking is illegal. Essentially a trafficker is a hustler, a pimp, a pirate, or have the propensities and tendencies to engage in these ungodly characteristics. The trafficker is looking for the pure, innocent, talented, qualified, and vulnerable to abuse, use, sell, and profit off of. This is what is happening in the spirit realm when someone uses your gift for personal benefits. They are using the purity, innocence, and vulnerability of who the person is for profit and gain.

Human traffickers are not concerned about the identity of the person. They actually strip the person of their identity through persuasion, coercion, seduction, terror, rape, or physical abuse. They feed off the person's weaknesses, desires, potential, and abilities. Even if the desires are healthy and necessary, the trafficker uses them to manipulate and seduce the person, while drawing them into the trafficking lifestyle.

Traffickers also use seducing, controlling and intimidating tactics to brainwash people into thinking that trafficking is all they are good for in life. As the person's identity is demoralized and stripped, they becomes a hollow shell with robotic qualities. They only respond to doing what they are told to do. If the person exudes any signs of still possessing identity or a sense of self, they are further intimidated, beaten and raped into submission. Such a person will sometimes submit due to fear of further abuse or dying. If they continue to challenge their traffickers, and demonstrate difficulty with submitting to the trafficking lifestyle, they are often killed in front of other trafficked persons (sacrificed), to instill the message that having identity is a *"no no"* in the trafficking world.

This is continuously occurring within the body of Christ. People fear not being used of God, being released in their calling, or fear being disloyal or displeasing to God, so they yield to spiritual traffickers. Some also have a desire for people, ministries, and regions to be blessed, so they yield to spiritual traffickers in hopes that people will be empowered, even though they are being disempowered.

I refer spiritual trafficking as the user spirit. The user spirit operates like a prostituting anointing, but unlike the trafficked person, the prostitute gets paid for their services. Most people impacted by the user spirit are not sufficiently honored with appropriate honorariums, nor are they appreciated and honored for the work they invested into people or an event. Scriptures are generally used to justify this behavior. But many of the scriptures that are speaking about being dishonored refer to:

- Those of the world's system
- Those who hate Jesus or do not want true gospel
- Those who are ignorant to the standards and operations of God's kingdom
- The religious and the Pharisees
- Those who operate in unbelief

If you claim not to be any of these, yet operate in dishonor and only engage people when you want something from them, you very well be a spiritual trafficker who is hustling the gifts and calling of saints for your own personal gain and prestige. Let take a moment to define dishonor.

Webster's Dictionary defines *dishonor* as:

1. lack of honor; disgrace; ignominy; shame; reproach
2. the nonpayment or nonacceptance of commercial paper by the party on whom it is drawn
3. to deprive of honor; to disgrace; to bring reproach or shame on; to treat with indignity, or as unworthy in the sight of others; to stain the character of
4. to lessen the reputation of; as, the duelist dishonors himself to maintain his honor
5. to violate the chastity of; to debauch (corrupt, pervert, seduce)
6. to refuse or decline to accept or pay; -- said of a bill, check, note, or draft which is due or presented; as, to dishonor a bill exchange

Sometimes dishonor is not done publicly, but privately through dealings and interactions. The operations of spiritual trafficking is done privately. It is conducted underhandedly and underground, within its own little realm and sphere of influence. So publicly a person can be accoladed where it appears as if they are being valued and honored, but privately, the world and operation of spiritual trafficking is alive and evident in their dealings. Saints need to be aware of this type of behavior in within the body of Christ. It is ungodly, wounding and humiliated.

David was constantly dishonored. He was used for his gifts but in his identity as a person.

> ***Psalms 62:4*** *They only consult to cast him down from his height [to dishonor him]; they delight in lies. They bless with their mouths, but they curse inwardly. Selah [pause, and calmly think of that]!*

The user spirit is a dishonoring and degrading spirit that makes a person and their ministry feel they are not worthy of the calling on their life, even though they are being used for their gifts and the anointing on their lives. Once used they are discarded and/or toss aside without any honor for how they poured out or invested their gifts, time, and life into that ministry endeavor.

This user spirit is a form of rejection. As to say we reject you or deem you not good enough, unworthy, irrelevant outside your gift. We accept what you can do but reject who you are. We accept your gift but reject, your identity and calling. Rejection is a characteristic of trafficking because it uses you, then dishonor you, refuse to acknowledge you, thinks it owns you, and can pull on you when it wants too. It trafficked your gift, while stripping your identity, and stealing the fruit and wealth that comes from your ordained identity.

With spiritual trafficking also comes the displacement of people from the alignment and will of God, as trafficking is the action or practice of illegally transporting people from one country or area to another. Typically for the purposes of forced labour or exploitation.

Dictionary.com defines exploitation as:
1. use or utilization, especially for profit
2. selfish utilization
3. to use selfishly for one's own ends

Some people are out of spiritual alignment because they have been seduced by spiritual traffickers who have coerced them to join their ministry, be a part of their event, come to their state and community to live and be a part of their ministry, etc. Many are being exploited and do not realize it. They are just happen to be a part of something, to belong, feel important, be utilized, or so they think is the case.

Some people operate as spiritual traffickers and know they are doing so. Some engage in trafficking ignorantly. They tend to operate in a respect of persons mindset, where they use a person or ministry for their gifts, while giving the platform ministers credit for the work, or taking the credit themselves.

Saints who have not been aware that they were apostles, may have been privy to being trafficked by leaders and ministries who use them for their gifts, but have not known or refuse to identify, mentor, and confirm them in their identity and calling. Such experiences can cause deep wounding to the person's identity and soul. Especially as they try to understand the reason they are embraced when they are being used for God's glory, then ostracized and rejected when the moment or event is over.

Laben Spiritually Trafficks Jacob

In *Genesis 30-31*, we find Laben spiritually trafficking Jacob. Laben used Jacob for his gifts to prosper, but did not care about Jacob's identity, destiny, or the generational lineage and heritage he was building for his family. Laben used Jacob's love for Rachel to traffick his gifts. Every time Jacob wanted to leave and take his family, and walk in his destiny, Laben would increase his wages so he had to remain and pay work off his debt. Jacob and his family had to eventually flee to rid himself of Laben. Even with Jacob being his son in law, Laben would not give him his blessing with SHIFTING into his true destiny and calling. Laben was angry that Jacob had fled. He attempted to make him feel guilty for not providing a proper goodbye. The trafficker will have you thinking you owe them respect and gratitude, even in your departure. They will not let you walk out the door, but will track you, and further inflict humiliation upon you because you left them.

Because of the many giftings of the apostle and the expansive anointing upon their lives, some people and ministries will pursue them for their gift, but will not want to honor them for their work. Apostles may also have the experience of being a part of works where spiritually they are governing the event, carrying the weight of the vision, ensuing all the warfare because of the vision, bringing forth deliverance and healing to attendees, and because the vision is successful, and their are people with greater platforms than the apostle, they are credited for the success of the vision. Whether intentional or unintentional, all of this is spiritual trafficking.

Moreover, apostles have to be careful because some leaders and ministries like to keep them around because of the anointing and mantle on their lives, while binding them to false loyalties that stifle their growth and success. Apostles gifts will produce and reproduce, but their mantles cannot flourish in environments that are not God designed. Like Jacob, the mantle will be dying, while the gifts are being trafficked for man's glory. They will not care if your identity is stripped and your mantle is dying, as long as their identity and ministry is flourishing at your expense. They will appear to care about you, but really all they care about is your gift, what they gain from it, and what they will loose if you leave. They may brainwash into believing you are loved, valued, and appreciated. But I decree you will be discerning of this seducing charismatic witchcraft. I decree you shall discern how their actions envy you, devalue you, and undermine your worth. That you will not yield to the lie that you are betraying them when you feel the union of the Holy Spirit to leave and that every unhealthy soultie and undermining of your identity will be exposed and thwarted in Jesus name. **SHIFT!**

Amnon Sexually Trafficks Tamar

In *2Samuel 13*, we find that Amnon sexually trafficked Tamar. The word tells us that Amnon loved Tamar. If you study the word love in this scripture, you will discern that this is not healthy love. The love he had for her was lustful, twisted and sadistic. It was fleshly love because of how beautiful and pure she was. He was so captivated in his own perversion that the love he had made him sick in lust for Tamar – he just had to have her.

Amnon took the advise of a friend, pretended to be ill, and encouraged his father to send Tamar to care for him. As she was tending to him upon his sickbed, he raped her. After raping her, he threw her away like a prostitute. She was so distraught that she tore her own mantle and lived desolate for the rest of her life. She never walked in destiny because the trafficker stripped her of her purity and identity.

Tamar did not want Amnon to throw her out. She was shamed and defiled and thus, deemed it better if he married her than to throw her away. Amnon's twisted impartation, tainted her identity where she would rather marry her rapist than to live with horrors what happened to her. If he married her then she could live in the false reality of considering his actions as love. But if he did not marry her, then she had to face the truth that she had been raped. Many sexually trafficked victims feel and behave the same way Tamar did. They are striving to cope with and justify the trauma that has occurred to their identity.

Sometimes, the trafficker is done with their victim and tells them they can leave. The victim so wounded that they beg to stay, or they leave, but do not return to family or to their region. They are either shamed by family and culture for what has occurred, or are bound by so much personal shame, they attempt to build a new life and identity, rather than returning to the one they had before being trafficked.

Sexual trafficking is rampant in the church. Many women are shunned for being pregnant with leadership's children or exposing leaders on this type of behavior, etc., while the leaders toss them aside and keep on ministering. Many woman attempt to get the leader to leave their wife and marry them. They are then scene as the home wrecker while the leader keeps being the godly overseer of the ministry. Youth are sexually trafficked and bound to secrecy. When they expose the leader, most everyone denies it and moves forward with church as usual. Those struggling with sexual sins or sexual identity issues are taken advantage of, further stripped of their purity, innocence, and purity and then ostracized for not being delivered or no longer having faith in the church or God. It is a horrid mess. Apostles must be watchful guardians in protecting the purity, innocence, and identity of the God's people.

The Church Spiritually Trafficks Paul
Paul speaks about the dishonor of trafficking he entailed from the Corinthian church:

> *2Corinthians 11:7-15 The Message Bible*
> *I wonder, did I make a bad mistake in proclaiming God's Message to you without asking for something in return, serving you free of charge so that you wouldn't be*

inconvenienced by me? It turns out that the other churches paid my way so that you could have a free ride. Not once during the time I lived among you did anyone have to lift a finger to help me out. My needs were always supplied by the Christians from Macedonia province. I was careful never to be a burden to you, and I never will be, you can count on it. With Christ as my witness, it's a point of honor with me, and I'm not going to keep it quiet just to protect you from what the neighbors will think. It's not that I don't love you; God knows I do. I'm just trying to keep things open and honest between us.

And I'm not changing my position on this. I'd die before taking your money. I'm giving nobody grounds for lumping me in with those money-grubbing "preachers," vaunting themselves as something special. They're a sorry ry bunch – pseudo-apostles, lying preachers, crooked workers – posing as Christ's agents but sham to the core. And no wonder! Satan does it all the time, dressing up as a beautiful angel of light. So it shouldn't surprise us when his servants masquerade as servants of God. But they're not getting by with anything. They'll pay for it in the end.

Though Paul was discussing the lack of financial blessings that was not given to him, he address the spiritual trafficking of the Corinthian church because of honor. They failed to adequately honor him. Their actions were continuous and was a point of error that required rebuke and correction. His reasons for not addressing this sooner was due to not wanting to burden the ministry and the saints, but also, he did not want to be associated with crooked preachers and false ministers, who only ministered for money and who took advantage of saints and ministries.

There are a host of powerful, healthy ministers within the body of Christ that are spiritually trafficked and allow it for the very reason Paul mentioned above. Most often they will not even address the being spiritually trafficked and some do not even realize it. Most of them have the mindset that God will provide their needs so they proceed in preaching the gospel with no expectation of financial gain and honor. As God leads us, we should preach the gospel whether people or ministers can pay us or not, however, we should not allow people to hustle and pimp us. I believe we mistake this type of behavior with **Mark 5:5-11**, where Jesus told the disciples to shake the dust off their feet as they are not received with evangelizing the lost. Yet this is very different than the spiritual trafficking I am speaking of. Jesus was talking about the lost, I am speaking about saints who are supposed to honor, care for, and esteem, the work of God and his ministers. They are receiving the word and the benefits of the work, while rejecting and dishonoring the minister.

- If the minister chooses not to take an honorarium, then that is their choice; however, people and ministries should be held accountable in honoring whatever business arrangement they initially agree to, and communicate when they need to change it.
- People and ministries should not be allowed to treat ministers as less important or valuable, because they are not a known platform preacher.
- People and ministries should not use ministers for their gifts, then steal God's glory by taking all the credit, when they did not do anything but

watch that minister and others labor for God.

> ***1 Corinthians 9:11-15 The Amplified Bible***
> *If we have sown [the seed of] spiritual good among you, [is it too] much if we reap from your material benefits? If others share in this rightful claim upon you, do not we [have a still better and greater claim]? However, we have never exercised this right, but we endure everything rather than put a hindrance in the way [of the spread] of the good news (the Gospel) of Christ.*

Do you not know that those men who are employed in the services of the temple get their food from the temple? And that those who tend the altar share with the altar [in the offerings brought]? [On the same principle] the Lord directed that those who publish the good news (the Gospel) should live (get their maintenance) by the Gospel.

But I have not made use of any of these privileges, nor am I writing this [to suggest] that any such provision be made for me [now]. For it would be better for me to die than to have anyone make void and deprive me of my [ground for] glorifying [in this matter].

Paul is saying that honoring in this nature is of God and that people and ministries should have a heart to bless ministers who invest their lives into them. They should possess the DNA of God our father whose nature is to bless and give. Paul is revealing this to them so that they correct this in their character and dealings with other ministers. As for himself, he is contending that he would rather die than to have someone honor him simply because he corrected them to do so. He did not want any relations with blessings coming through false honor or a spirit of obligation. Paul was revealing that this type of spiritual trafficking is a heart matter. And since their hearts where not postured to esteem him, or to want him blessed by what God was doing through him and for all of them as a whole, they could keep their provision.

It is sad that Paul had to have this conversation with saints that he poured his life and ministry into, but truth is, this occurs often within the body of Christ. Paul had a right to be challenged by this behavior and to bring correction to it. It was his duty as an apostle and a leader. And even as a fellow saint within the body of Christ. We should never want to dishonor one another. **Philippians 2:3-5** tells us to,

> *Do nothing from factional motives [through contentiousness, strife, selfishness, or for unworthy ends] or prompted by conceit and empty arrogance. Instead, in the true spirit of humility (lowliness of mind) let each regard the others as better than and superior to himself [thinking more highly of one another than you do of yourselves].*
>
> *Let each of you esteem and look upon and be concerned for not [merely] his own interests, but also each for the interests of others. Let this same attitude and purpose and [humble] mind be in you which was in Christ Jesus: [Let Him be your example in humility:]*

We should humbly honor one another higher than we do ourselves. We should never give or treat anyone else less than we would ourselves. **SHIFT!**

Breaking Patterns of Spiritual Trafficking

For those who may have a background of rejection, abandonment, abuse, bullying, dishonor may have followed you throughout your life. As you examine your youth, you may notice patterns of dishonor. And as you have become saved and a minister of the gospel, the enemy uses the open doors of the saints to further dishonor and traffick you. It is important to break this curse in warfare and intercession and close doors to how it has tracked, trafficked, and dishonored you. Break the strongholds of illegal slavery, fraud, abuse, exploitation, coercion and every way you are used for your purity, innocence, and identity. Decree out who you are in God, and command that due honor be bestowed upon your life. Be cognizant of future endeavors and how people and ministries would attempt to traffick you. Ask God for wisdom on how to expose and correct these matters, and only co-labor with these ministries if God is requiring it. Approaching it as God designs allows you to be all things to all people, without succumbing to their schemes, or agreeing with their ungodly character and practices. As you remain your true identity, souls are saved for the sake of the gospel, and not to please, validate or yield to the traffickings of man.

> ***1Corinthians 9:18-19*** *What is my reward then? Verily that, when I preach the gospel, I may make the gospel of Christ without charge, that I abuse not my power in the*

gospel. For though I be free from all men, yet have I made myself servant unto all, that I might gain the more.

Verse 22-23 *To the weak became I as weak, that I might gain the weak: I am made all things to all men, that I might by all means save some. And this I do for the gospel's sake, that I might be partaker thereof with you.* **SHIFT!**

PURPOSE OF ORDINATION

I chose to write on this topic because there is a lot of mixed emotions and messages regarding being ordained. Many have the mindset of "*I do not need a title.*" But truthfully you would not want someone operating on you that did not have training, experience, and certified accreditation. Many use their title to control and abuse others and there are some are validated by their title. Then there are the ones that are sinful and lack the character and nature of God until you want to strip them of their title. They have made it difficult for those of us who are humble and integral in wearing the label of the Lord.

We cannot allow personal insecurities and the challenge of being associate with those who misuse titles to shame or hinder us from wanting and pursing ordination. If people who are truly submitted to God's will do not assert their right to be licensed and ordained then how will the world know who the truth Godly leaders are. We trying to hide when we should be at the forefront of the body of Christ and kingdom boldly declaring with our lives, "this is what God's leader looks like." We have to stop allowing the discrepancies of some shame us into shining the very gospel we claim we love, serve, and live for.

As you grow in God, being rewarded with licenses, ordinations, and certifications is a part of your reward. This is something God told me when I was being ordained. He said I was being rewarded and honored for my hard work and years of service, dedication, and maturity in him. He said he was proud of me and it was a moment to be proud of myself. When we are in the worldly educational system or in our jobs, we obtain degrees, certificates, awards, certifications, and bonuses for our progress and success. This should be the same within the body of Christ. We should want to honor and reward those who are fighting the good fight of faith. We keep making people believe that they are sacrificing their lives and no blessings or honor comes with that - that it is our duty to serve God. But God's entire bible and even one of the main reasons he creates is was so he could bless us. Jesus came so that we could be restored in the blessings of eternal life. We have to SHIFT from making this walk be all about dread and sacrifice and demonstrate the empowerment, grace, and productivity of the true kingdom of God.

> *Matthew 10:1-8 And when he had called unto him his twelve disciples, he gave them power against unclean spirits, to cast them out, and to heal all manner of sickness and all manner of disease. Now the names of the twelve apostles are these; The first, Simon, who is called Peter, and Andrew his brother; James the son of Zebedee, and John his brother; Philip, and Bartholomew; Thomas, and Matthew the publican; James the son of Alphaeus, and Lebbaeus, whose surname was Thaddaeus; Simon the Canaanite, and Judas Iscariot, who also betrayed him. These twelve Jesus sent forth, and commanded them, saying, Go not into the way of the Gentiles, and into any city of the Samaritans enter ye not: But go rather to the lost sheep of the house of Israel. And as ye go, preach, saying, The kingdom of heaven is at hand. Heal the sick, cleanse the lepers, raise the dead, cast out devils: freely ye have received, freely give.*

> *Luke 6:10-12 And it came to pass in those days, that he went out into a mountain to pray, and continued all night in prayer to God. And when it was day, he called unto him his disciples: and of them he chose twelve, whom also he named apostles; Simon, (whom he also named Peter,) and Andrew his brother, James and John, Philip and Bartholomew, Matthew and Thomas, James the son of Alphaeus, and Simon called Zelotes, And Judas the brother of James, and Judas Iscariot, which also was the traitor.*

Ordination sets you a part as a forerunner of the gospel of Jesus Christ. It distinguishes you, defines your anointing and calling. Jesus appointed 12 apostles even though he had an abundance of disciples.

Ordination reveals your rank and authority over principalities and powers and your supernatural abilities.

Ordination helps establish and solidify the specific work, vision, and focus regarding the calling and mantle that is upon your life.

The apostles did not realize they were ready to be leaders. They we're still striving to walk in the shadow of Jesus. But Jesus was trying to get them to make their own shadow. They were still trying to be disciples and operate among the familiar where they were still fascinated by the power of God when Jesus has set them a part to know they had all power and authority to perform greater works.

> *Luke 10:17:20 And the seventy returned again with joy, saying, Lord, even the devils are subject unto us through*

> *thy name. And he said unto them, I beheld Satan as lightning fall from heaven. Behold, I give unto you power to tread on serpents and scorpions, and over all the power of the enemy: and nothing shall by any means hurt you. Notwithstanding in this rejoice not, that the spirits are subject unto you; but rather rejoice, because your names are written in heaven.*

Ordination will expose your motives and level of submissiveness for following Jesus. The apostles did not know that were truly submitted to Jesus until they were faced with being on the front line and declaring whether he was the Messiah. Because they were still operated as disciples, they denied, betrayed, and abandoned Jesus, while others hid from the persecution of Jesus. They had hands on training, commissioning and personal confirming from Jesus that they were apostles, but did not realize it was time to walk in it. After Jesus resurrected, they realized their lives were no longer business as usual.

If the apostles could have walked in Jesus shadow forever they would have. But Jesus said in **Matthew 9:36**, *"Then saith he unto his disciples, The harvest truly is plenteous, but the labourers are few."* Jesus did not need a fan club. He needed laborers for the gospel. He needed some ambassadors, some trailblazers, some miracle workers, some KINGDOM SHIFTERS!

Some people receive all type of training, attend limitless conferences, is at every church event, have a consistent study and prayer life, are fervent in the things of the Lord, but they hide behind their leaders or behind religious church duties and experiences. They idolize the presence and work of the Lord, yet do not realize that this dangerous or that it grieves Jesus. Licensing and ordination SHIFTS them out of hiding and into the forefront where they belong.

When God revealed to me that I was an apostle and I was resistant to embracing the title, he begin to show me how some of my warfare was the enemy taking advantage of the fact that I had not become my ultimate identity in the earth and that I had not been set in that position. He told me that I needed to position myself to be ordained. See the enemy will take your position, your land, your realms, your regions, your authority, your rewards, your blessings, and whatever else you reject or refuse to claim. He knows you own it so this is his way of recapturing it. He knows your love for God but sees your fears and insecurities. He uses that to combat you for what could be yours if you just claim it.

Apostolic ministry is not traditional church. It is equipping school. It is for the perfecting of the saints. That means you are trained and educated in the things of God. You then graduate and go forth in demonstrating what you learned, while having seasons of obtaining more knowledge and maturity, and being released again as a laborer of Jesus.

> ***Ephesians 4:11-13*** *And he gave some, apostles; and some, prophets; and some, evangelists; and some, pastors and teachers; For the perfecting of the saints, for the work of the ministry, for the edifying of the body of Christ: Till we all come in the unity of the faith, and of the knowledge of the Son of God, unto a perfect man, unto the measure of the stature of the fulness of Christ.*

Ephesians 1:17-18 *that the God of our Lord Jesus Christ, the Father of glory, may give to you a spirit of wisdom and of revelation in the knowledge of Him. I pray that the eyes of your heart may be enlightened, so that you will know what is the hope of His calling, what are the riches of the glory of His inheritance in the saints.*

Colossians 1:9-10 *For this reason also, since the day we heard of it, we have not ceased to pray for you and to ask that you may be filled with the knowledge of His will in all spiritual wisdom and understanding, so that you will walk in a manner worthy of the Lord, to please Him in all respects, bearing fruit in every good work and increasing in the knowledge of God.*

1Peter 2:2 *Like newborn babies you should crave (thirst for, earnestly desire) the pure (unadulterated) spiritual milk, that by it you may be nurtured and grow unto [completed] salvation.*

2Peter 3:17-18 *You therefore, beloved, knowing this beforehand, be on your guard so that you are not carried away by the error of unprincipled men and fall from your own steadfastness, but grow in the grace and knowledge of our Lord and Savior Jesus Christ To Him be the glory, both now and to the day of eternity. Amen.*

Wisdom Keys For Aligning With Ordination

- Unless God requires, do not submit to a ministry that does not have an established vision plan to train, mentor, license, ordain, and release saints in their calling. The Holy Spirit is going to put you in school whether man does or not. You have a choice and a right to be aligned with what Jesus is doing in your life.

- If you are a part of a ministry and they keep promising to train, mentor, license, and ordained but never follow through, seek God on whether you can transition to a ministry that has these qualities. If the ministry and it leaders are too busy to make provision for them they are stuck in Works and not in kingdom business. At your job, there are required trainings you must have to fulfill policy. Some trainings align you with promotions and look good on your resume for other positions. The church has to SHIFT in fulfilling the word of the Lord regarding equipping and releasing saints. If it is not a part of the vision then religion, laziness, or poor vision at work. God is not requiring you to submit to any of these without purpose.

- If you are at a ministry that trains, license, or ordains, but does not provide or create platform for you to be utilized or assist you in identifying your well of release so you can joining the labors of God, then explore if you should be their. Who obtains a doctorate and do not utilize it? That's right, "NO ONE!" You will die and suffocate sitting on the pew full of knowledge and equipping that is dormant. Every minute you yield to this is every minute your destiny is dying. A lot of times leaders will say it is your character or this or that. But they are your leader. They should be helping to receive deliverance and healing so you can progress in God. I am not talking to apostles who are out of order. I am talk to those who genuinely are going through the proper channels yet dying on the pews.

- Also please note that as apostles, God will release vision for work. If you are at a ministry that has no vision beyond the four walls of the church and operating in the mundane "RUN!" We'll ask God if you can "RUN!" Especially if they do not release you to empower a team to fulfill that work or release you to go and complete that assignment. Again I am not speaking to those with character issues and the like. I am talking to those who are ready in spirit and character to labor for the Lord.

A SHIFT occurs when you are being licensed or ordained. The apostles were SHIFTED into a season of warfare due to SHIFT in their calling and did not even know it. Jesus said the following to Peter.

> **Luke 22:31-34 The Amplified Bible** *Simon, Simon (Peter), listen! Satanhas asked excessively that [all of] you be given up to him [out of the power and keeping of God], that he might sift [all of] you like grain, But I have prayed especially for you [Peter], that your [own] faith may not fail; and when you yourself have turned again, strengthen and establish your brethren. And [Simon Peter] said to Him, Lord, I am ready to go with You both to prison and to death. But Jesus said, I tell you, Peter, before a [single] cock shall crow this day, you will three times [utterly] deny that you know Me.*

Peter thought he was ready for this SHIFT but it was Jesus who was interceding for him. It is important to have a support system interceding for you when being in a season of licensing, ordination, or elevation. The devil will come for your truth, identity, faith, and stability. He wants you to think you are not prepared for the SHIFT. You ready for the work and call, you just were not expecting that warfare. Peter had his guard down, but Jesus was discerning. Peter will still operating like a passionate disciple instead of a zealous apostle. Those interceding for you will help you navigate through this SHIFT successfully. Peter made a mistake but he did not abort his calling because he had protection and covering. He was able to repent, SHIFT and move forward in his destiny and calling.

After I was ordained, I felt numb. I did not know how to process what had occurred. There were so many thoughts going on in my heart and spirit. The warfare around me was intense and the fiery darts from naysayers confounded the experience. It was my supports that helped to keep me balanced, encouraged me to celebrate, celebrated me, and continually reminded me that I had already been doing the work - I was already an apostle. But was laboring and unveiling from an elevated dimension.

Being ordained for me has been like learning myself all over again from a new magnitude. It has been fun but trying. It has been liberating but tedious. I believe it is because I ended one very long 12 year assignment and started another one. And now it is my ministry I am pioneering and trailblazing. Whewwww! That will be a future book - to be continued.

Whatever your experience is, embrace aligning yourself with licensing, ordination, and continual upward mobility and success. You deserve every reward and all the spoils of war that will unfold on your path. Blessings to your calling, your mantle, and your journey with God! Wear that mantle well! **SHIFT!**

APOSTOLIC REFRESHING PRAYER

I love you Lord Jesus. I thank you for who you are. I thank you for all you do. I thank you for choosing me, loving me, and journey as one sound, one heart beat, one spirit with me.

I enmesh with you all the more Jesus. I decree I am intricately in tune and consumed inside your presence and the very foundation of my being is your throne room.

I repent for any sins in my life and any way I have operated in my own strength and not through the power and authority of the calling and mantle upon my life. Even as I cleanse through the blood of Jesus, I decree a SHIFT back under the wings of your glory, under my mantle - your covering.

I rebuke all fear, inadequacy, hardship, pain from persecution, rejection, bitterness, anger, resentment, confusion, bewitchment, instability, and affliction sent to stagnate and drain me of my time, attention, and healthiness. I loose the snatching power of God to pluck these ungodly attributes up out of the foundation, heart, soul, and mind of my life, and I kick out every spirit operating with and in these unhealthy entities.

I decree refreshing to myself, my identity, my mantle, my calling, my destiny. I am refreshing and renewing even now. I decree Proverbs. 11:25 is my portion and as I generously water others, I am immediately and continuously watered in the glory of God.

Thank you God for your refreshing. Thank you for wisdom to know when I need refreshing. Thank you for your Holy Spirit that revives me, replenishes me, and equips me to live a balanced life poured out for your glory. **SHIFT!**

APOSTOLIC DISCIPLINES FOR WELLNESS & REFRESHING

Apostles live a life of readiness - dedicated to God. They have to live a disciplined life of a soldier because there warfare is daily so their discipline must be daily. Apostles must love disciplined. They must love to live refreshed and ready in completing the work of the kingdom. Living and demonstrating exemplarity sonship as an ambassador of Jesus. The Apostle's lifestyle identity is one that is ready to represent, establish, and advance, the image, kingdom, will, and plan of God in the earth.

> *Luke 12:35-38 Be dressed in readiness, and keep your lamps lit. Be like men who are waiting for their master when he returns from the wedding feast, so that they may immediately open the door to him when he comes and knocks. Blessed are those slaves whom the master will find on the alert when he comes; truly I say to you, that he will gird himself to serve, and have them recline at the table, and will come up and wait on them. Whether he comes in the second watch, or even in the third, and finds them so, blessed are those slaves.*
>
> *2Corinthians 10:6 And having in a readiness to revenge all disobedience, when your obedience is fulfilled.*
>
> *2Timothy 4:2 Preach the word; be instant in season, out of season; reprove, rebuke, exhort with all longsuffering and doctrine.*
>
> *2Corinthians 4:16-18 The Amplified Bible Therefore we do not become discouraged (utterly spiritless, exhausted, and wearied out through fear). Though our*

outer man is [progressively] decaying and wasting away, yet our inner self is being [progressively] renewed day after day. For our light, momentary affliction (this slight distress of the passing hour) is ever more and more abundantly preparing and producing and achieving for us an everlasting weight of glory [beyond all measure, excessively surpassing all comparisons and all calculations, a vast and transcendent glory and blessedness never to cease!], since we consider and look not to the things that are seen but to the things that are unseen; for the things that are visible are temporal (brief and fleeting), but the things that are invisible are deathless and everlasting.

Apostles must Implementing the following keys to live a life refreshed and ready:

Consistent Prayer Life
- Apostolic soldiers are born and breezed as weapons of destruction in the essence of Jesus.
- Identity and continual evolving of self is birthed in prayer.
- One's calling and mantled is supernaturally commissioned in the engulfment of Jesus
- Rank and authority is confirmed and increased in prayer.
- Spirit gifts are supernaturally endured inside the power of Jesus.
- The fruit, character, nature of God, and a relationship with the Holy Spirit is conceived and nurtured in prayer.
- Revelation and books for publishing are conceived in intimacy with Jesus.
- Warfare strategies are revealed in prayer
- Refreshing and renewal comes through communion

in Jesus.
- Empowerment is awakened in prayer
- Vision is illuminated and consummated inside the presence of Jesus.
- Maturity is produced in prayer.
- Acceleration and advancement is imparted through the consumption of Jesus.
- Zeal is infused and resurrected in prayer
- Deliverance, healing, breakthrough, miracles, and wholeness is generating in the magnificence of Jesus.
- Holiness righteousness, purity, and virtue is imparted and nurtured in prayer.
- Boldness, confidence and unwavering faith is solidified through devotion with Jesus.

- Fasting and Consecration
- Apostles should live a life of fasting and consecration. I generally fast two to three times a week. Sometimes I do water only, water and pure juices only, and other times I may do veggies and water only. You have to do what is best for you and what God says. He may give you a more or less stringent lifestyle regimen of fasting.
- When I do extended fasts (21 days, 40 days), I have someone outside the ministry interceding for me. They help to fortify me in the safety of God so the enemy does not use my fasting to cause affliction. I deal with constant warfare of affliction so this helps to close me in.
- I do not fast when I am on the battle ground - when I am on a ministry assignment. I usually fast beforehand. Soldiers in the natural do not fast when they are at war. There bodies need

nourishment and protein to remain energized and strengthened. They fast ahead of time and eat lots of healthy food to build their energy when in battle. So unless the Lord leads me, I do not fast on the battleground, I fast beforehand.
- Fasts and consecration should always have a purpose and focus where tangible fruit is evident within and at the end of this time of communing and sacrifice.

Study Of The Word
- **2Timothy 2:15** *Study to shew thyself approved unto God, a workman that needeth not to be ashamed, rightly dividing the word of truth.*
- Apostles become a walking bible - a sign and a wonder - when they feast on the word.
- Apostles are able to preach, teach and impart sound doctrine when studying their word.
- Apostles are able to lay biblical foundations and combat unbiblical foundations and falsehoods when they feast on the word.
- Apostles can manifest the kingdom with signs following when they consistent digest the word.

Be Ye Holy
- **1Peter 1:15** *But just as he who called you is holy, so be holy in all you do.*
- Apostles must be holiness or hell; the must reject being lukewarm and full of mixture.
- Apostles must Love and intensely pursue virtue, holiness, righteousness and purity.

Vision Minded
- Unless the Lord leads apostles must resist works that lack vision and clear biblical foundation.

- Apostles must have clear Apostolic vision and fervently operating on it and in it
- Apostles must pray for vision and clarity in being able to articulate and impart that vision into others.
- Works without vision will be draining for the apostle and an open door for unnecessary warfare.

Cautious of Sifting & Draining Spirits
- Apostles must be unapologetic about being focused in the matters of God and not allowing people, the devil, the common, mediocre, the form and fashion, and the worldly, to drain, distract, traffick and sift their gifts and calling (Remember Apostle Peter was in jeopardy to be sifted as wheat by the devil but Jesus interceded for him).

Communing In The Night Season
- Apostles must trust God to refresh and restore them when they are being assumed to the night watches. Sleeping when God is unctioning you to pray will drain and weary the apostle. Sluggardness and laziness will enter in to further oppress and release slack to the readiness of the apostle.
- The apostle must commune and cultivate their spirits at night by sleeping to soaking music, worship music and scriptures.
- Apostles must go to bed meditating upon Jesus, his word, his goodness.
- Apostles must ask for and pursue divine visitations from Jesus, the Holy Spirit and Angels at night.

Times of Refreshing
- Praise and worship is the most sacred gift an apostle have for quickly refreshing in God's presence. Even a few seconds or minutes of praise

and worship can empower the apostle. Especially if they have cultivated a lifestyle of this. The Holy Spirit will immediately activate and comfort the apostle. Apostles walk by the spirit - by the knowing of God. Sometimes you may not feel his presence but you will know it has encompassed and infused you.

- Soaking in the Holy Spirit and the fruit of the Holy Spirit. Sometimes I just sit and soak myself in God's love, his joy, his peace, his truth, his blood. I just fill up on him, feast on him, commune with him. I am not focused on feeling but in knowing God is gracing me with what I need to strengthen and resurrect me. I do this in the car, elevator, walking down the street, on my bed at night. Whenever I need Holy Spirit I commune with him as friend.
- Speaking in fierce tongues. Using your prayer language is one of the quickest ways the apostle can be supernaturally energized. Speaking in fierce Holy Spirit tongues (not mumbling) SHIFTS you quickly into the spirit, bypassing your mind and emotions and earthly things. It also serves as a cleansing to the heart and soul, while helping to edify you in areas you are waning.
- Apostles must immediately surrender all worries, challenges, stressors, persecutions, offenses and insecurities to God; as you end your day verbally release these matters to God and then meditate upon his goodness, scriptures and yield to praise and worship.
- Apostles must take time away from the crowd to by quiet, still away with the Lord and just be for a while. You can do this for an hour, thirty minutes, a day, etc. It is important to be cognizant of needing this and taking this time for yourself, especially

since you live a life poured out. You are an open vessel of water to others, you have to be protective of making sure you replenish. Jesus always stole away to refresh. Those small moments of refreshing will keep you zealous and ready, while fortifying you against burnout and battle fatigue.

Embracing Respite
- Apostles have to know when to take breaks to enjoy life, replenish, be delivered and healed, rejuvenated, and invigorated with fresh vision. This can be a week, two weeks, even a month. God will lead you. When he does, SHIFT responsibilities to those under you and rest. Or just trust that if God is leading you, all will be well when you return.
- Have scheduled times to replenish and apostle days where you just "be" for a day. Monday's is my "Taquetta" day. I rest from ministry and do whatever I want. You might cannot take a whole day but schedule you some time where it is just for you - all about you. This will close doors where the enemy will make you feel taken for granted and where you may feel like there is no time for you as your life is all about Jesus. This is a very human and understandable feeling so include balance and include appreciation of yourself in your walk.

Recognizing Battle Fatigue
- Battle fatigue is an actual psychological disorder.
- It's symptoms include anxiety, depression, loss of motivation, slowed reaction time, indecision, caused by the stress and trauma of active warfare.
- Combat fatigue or shell shock is psychological disorder where the person experiences a loss of sight, memory, etc, resulting from psychological

- strain during prolonged engagement in warfare.
- Battle and combat fatigue can also include post traumatic stress disorder. Symptoms include traumatization, stuck in a place of shock and awe from experiences, becoming numb in one's thoughts and persistent reliving traumatic experiences in ones' thoughts, eye gates, imagination, and dreams.
- Deliverance, counseling and a process of healing is needed should you become battle fatigued. Do not rely on self deliverance in this instance. Some of your body systems and emotions have shut down within this disorder. You will not possess the emotional strength to SHIFT yourself into complete wholeness. Pride will also try to rule you and make you think you are okay and do not need help. Pride is dangerous to an apostle. Pride will cause you to operate in your human intellect and strength rather than the spirit of God. You will begin to make mistakes because you have SHIFTED from u see your mantle. Remember your mantle is what enables you to carrying, operate in and sustain in your calling. The quicker you surrender to the process, the faster you can return to your apostolic duties.

Recognizing Burnout
(Excerpt from Taquetta's Book Healing The Wounded Leader)
Burn out is when a apostle needs a time of rest and consecration, but refuses to take it due to false or delusional obligations and loyalties to God and the people; Often there is a fear associated with the false obligations and loyalties, such as fear that someone will take their position while they are resting.

When an apostle is burned out they flow through the wells of bitterness, anger, verbal aggression, intimidation and control. This is because:

- They are extremely tired and drained physically, emotionally and spiritually.
- They are operating on fumes and have nothing to give.
- Tiredness causes them to be easily angered and frustrated even by minor things.
- They are irritable, negative, skeptical, and pessimistic.
- They lack temperance, and patience, while being overly critical and insensitive in their leading style.
- They feel justified in their actions as they have taken on a disposition that they have to do everything themselves, because nothing gets done properly without them.

It is important for apostles to recognize the signs of burnout and take time to refresh and restore themselves as when they do not acknowledge this, burnout can result in wounding others while further wounding themselves.

Burnout can cause unhealthy, emotional and abrupt decision making that can wound and even abort the vision of the ministry. When apostles are not willing to take time to refresh and be delivered and healed, they have become an idol to the people and the vision. They carry the burden of the people and ministry rather operating through the spirit and strength of God.

Discerning Burnout: Lets conduct a burnout check as this is essential for knowing when respite, deliverance and healing is needed.

- *Stress* - feeling strained, weighted, burdened by life and one's responsibilities; experiencing a physical pressure or pull, while having to exert force or energy to engage in the day and to complete tasks.
- *Exhaustion* - feeling tired all the time. The tiredness can be felt in your body, mind and emotions. Experiencing restlessness and thought racing while trying to sleep; attempting oversleep in effort to compensate for tiredness, yet increase sleep does not break the exhaustion.
- *Dissatisfied With Life* - Wearied while displaying impatience and dissatisfaction even with things that should bring joy and pleasure. Difficult to enjoy things due to exhaustion and weariness.
- *Emotional Imbalance* - Easily irritated, frustrated, and angered. Feel a lack of self-worth or unappreciated. Experience loneliness, emptiness, resentment, and as if you have to do everything even though help is available to you. Experience double mindedness, pessimism, and is plagued with negative thoughts about life, people, and responsibilities. There is a heaviness upon the heart and body in the form of depression and grief. There can be crying for no reason or a feeling of wanting to cry but the tears do not flow.
- **False Obligation and Loyalty** - There is a sense of false obligation and loyalty to complete tasks and take on tasks that are not of immediate important. There is a false obligation and loyalty to follow through with duties even when others are

offering assistance or when others recognize you need rest. This is pride at work.
- ***Lack of Motivation*** - Do not desire to engage in day to day activities. Difficulty getting out of bed, progressing forward with the day. There can also be a dragging through the day accompanied by enthusiasm, ability to encourage self or be encouraged. At times there will be surge of strength exerted by will power, but then this strength will be zapped by the reality of burnout.
- ***Distraction*** - Difficulty concentrating, focusing, remembering things, problem solving, making important decisions, leading others, while being easily distracted by plaguing negative thoughts, weariness, and the fact of being exhausted and not having anything to give.
- ***Lack of Self Care*** - Stop eating right, exercising, praying, spending time with God, studying your bible, equipping self in one's gifting and calling, vacationing, taking weekly personal days, spending time with family and friends, grooming self to one's taste and standards.
- ***Unhealthy Coping Mechanisms*** - Resort to drinking, drugs, smoking, overeating, under eating, poor eating habits, self-medicating by taking sleeping pills or pills for energy, inordinate sex acts, engaging in risky or unhealthy behaviors and activities.
- ***Relationship and Family Issues*** - Exhibiting poor coping, conflict resolution, communication, anger management, relational, and social skills. Difficulty receiving and giving constructive criticism; easily offended, while harboring unforgiveness, bitterness, retaliation and resentment.

- *Unhealthy Boundaries* - Not being discerning in one's relationships and interactions. Becoming more than God is requiring to those in need or those you counsel, mentor or shepherd. Engaging in unhealthy emotional ties. Have a need to fix, rescue, or Lord over a person or task. Becoming sexually attracted, sexually engaging, and/or getting personal or emotional needs met in relationships and interactions that are not with a person that is your wife or husband.
- *Moral Discrepancies* - Exhibiting behaviors that is out of your character and standards, and is definitely not the character or nature of God. (e.g. yelling at people, being combative, disruptive, yielding to sin, risking public reproach, ministering through issues and through personal perceptions while causing harm or challenges for others).
- *Poor Performance Level* - Feel as if you are giving your all, but work ethic is not up to par; duties and responsibilities consume your mind and thoughts, but you really are not getting much accomplished due to sluggardness and burnout. There is a downgrade to your performance compared to when you are refreshed and balanced in your day to day activities. Even if a goal is achieved, you recognize that it was not your best and/or that it took more energy, focus, work ethic and time than necessary.
- **Health Problems** - Experience stress related health problems (e.g. headaches, stomach aches, ulcers, digestive issues, respiratory infections, depression, anxiety, heart issues, addictions).

When you are burnout, you should take respite immediately to refresh. You may also need deliverance, healing, counseling and a process to wholeness if you have been experiencing burnout for an extended period of time.

Identifying Woundedness
- Hurts, offense, tears, ungodly roots and fruits in the soul, heart, mind, will, and emotions.
- Displaying public and private sin issues, ungodly lusts, character flaws, and discrepancies
- Trouble sleeping, anxious, restless
- Instability will be evident in the apostle's words, thought processing, emotions and actions. The bible called this double mindedness. Depending on the symptoms, the counseling arena calls this bipolar disorder, major depression or schizophrenia. Usually, but not always the case, a wounded apostle that is unstable, is battling internal warfare with themselves, their generations, and/or sometimes with God.
- Blaming all warfare on the devil or people, when you have open doors
Easily offended, angered, and have the potential to wound and murder others with your words and deeds.
- Manifesting demons and characteristics of rage, anger, rejection, rebellion, inferiority, insecurity, unworthiness, abuse, unhealthiness
- Experiencing sicknesses and afflictions
- Feel taken for granted or taken advantage of
- Full of excuses.
- Resistant and disobedient in following through with tasks or completing the work of the Lord
- Want to punish and retaliate against people or the vision.

- Displaying delusion, bewitchment, forgetfulness, spaciness
- Prideful, false sense of self, stealing God's glory, and stealing the spoils of war that really are a reproach and sin against God. Taking credit for the things God and people perform, or refuse to award or accolade anyone who they fear will receive more glory and praise than them.

Choose Your Battles Wisely
- Every battle is not for you as the apostle to fight.
- Though equipped, apostles must know what battles are theirs to fight.
- Fighting battles that God did not orchestrate causes unnecessary hardship, warfare, wounds, stress, and tiredness.
- David asked God should he fight a battle: **2Samuel 5-19** *And David inquired of the LORD, saying, Shall I go up to the Philistines? wilt thou deliver them into mine hand? And the LORD said unto David, Go up: for I will doubtless deliver the Philistines into thine hand.*
- The devil, witches, wicked and worldly people will provoke you to battle.
- Witches, warlocks, principalities and powers will attack you just for coming in their region, on their land, in their store, etc. You have to discern if it is a battle God is giving you or should you just let it be. There are times where I am literally saying out loud, "I am not hear to battle." Usually demons, witches, etc. back up off me and release me of whatever spells etc. they have unleashed. If the do not then you can assert authority over them but do not go into an all out war. This is essential as the more you grow in your authority, the more the

demonic realm will identify you and seek to pounce you before you attack them. You not trying to fight demons on vacations, rest days, while you trying to buy something at Walmart, etc. If you lash out every time you feel witchcraft and oppression, you will be fighting wars all day everyday. And you will be fighting from your emotions and from being appalled that demons and witches recognized and attacked you, rather than from strategy from Jesus.
- Wise warriors wins battles and obtain the spoils, while still being healthy for the next battle.

Utilize Your Supports
- Apostolic ministry is team ministry.
- Apostles empower groups of people for the work of the kingdom. Though they have the ability to wear many hats, they do not do everything themselves. Apostles empower and train their team to help carry the vision.
- Apostles have a small support team that personally assist them with day to day life endeavors. These people have a heart for them where they intercede, serve, complete tasks, supply needs, sow financially and through blessings, etc. Ask God to reveal these people to you. Be open to leaning on them and allowing them to be who God need them to be to you in warfare, intercession, support, and servanthood.

APOSTOLIC HEALING PRAYER

I decree God's deliverance and healing power to your identity, calling and apostolic journey. I decree that you are embracing your identity and calling as an apostle and that you are SHIFTING out of woundedness, rejection, dread, and hatred for what and who God has called you to be in the earth. I decree the spirit of Abba father is mounting you as you accept that you are called! Jesus appointed you, Jesus has need of you, and though he will send others to confirm, empower, equip and release you in the calling upon your life, he is SHIFTING you through his "sent one" anointing, to walk confidently in your apostolic journey with him. I decree that you will embrace the divine connections, mentoring, and covering he has for you, and that you will know by his spirit and fruit who is of him and who is a pawn for the enemy. I decree divine strategic eternal success as you walk boldly as an apostle. I decree you will be innately rooted, grounded, and balanced in the character, nature, principles, standards, fruit, signs, wonders, will, and plans of the Lord, while being able to freely impart and establish these attributes into people, ministries, businesses, organizations, communities, regions, and nations. Even as holiness is still right and hell is very real, I decree your daily life will be a representation of the word of God, such that demons tremble and flee, principalities and powers are displaced, and people are uncomfortable in their sin and self and worldly ordained lifestyles and identities. MAY you always SHIFT people, ministries, businesses, strategic works, regions, and nations, while transforming lives, lands, climates, and atmospheres for God's Glory. **SHIFT!**

FEARLESS IMMOVABLE DECREE!

- Flesh do not move me
- Bad attitudes do not move me
- Intimidating and defying tactics of Goliath don't move me
- Jezebel's seductive and raging rants do not move me
- Backstabbing words and actions do not move me
- Betrayal do not move me
- Gossip, slander, and demonic chatter do not move me
- Misunderstandings and misjudgments; even when people just do not get it, get me - that does not move me
- Ridicule does not move me
- Lies do not move me
- False or manipulating burdens do not move me
- Rejection and the rejection issues of others do not move me
- Hatred. jealousy, competition, and covetousness does not move me
- Abandonment and people leaving do not move me
- Having to be lonely and journey in God alone does not move me
- Witches and witchcraft do not move me
- Demonic floods, winds, and storms do not move me
- Warfare and demonic visitations do not move me
- Trials, tribulation and persecution do not move me
- Devils and angry principalities and powers show do not move me
- The hounds of hell do not move me and can't stop me
-

- Death and being a martyr for Christ do not move me

  - ❖ I am fixed in God
  - ❖ I am secure in God
  - ❖ I am stable in God
  - ❖ I am moored in God
  - ❖ I am anchored in God
  - ❖ I am rooted in God
  - ❖ I am braced in God
  - ❖ I am set firm in God
  - ❖ I am steadfast in God
  - ❖ I am unbudgable in God
  - ❖ I am motionless in God
  - ❖ I am unmoving in God
  - ❖ I am immobile in God
  - ❖ I am stationary in God
  - ❖ I am at peace in God
  - ❖ I am still in God
  - ❖ I am stock-still in God
  - ❖ I am not moving a muscle in God
  - ❖ I am transfixed in God
  - ❖ I am paralyzed in God
  - ❖ I am frozen in God
  - ❖ I am fastened in God
  - ❖ I am locked in God
  - ❖ I am unwavering in God

BOOK REFERENCES

- *Blueletterbible.com*
- *Olivetree.com*
- *Wikipedia*
- *Dictionary.com*
- *Biblestudytools.com*
- *Spurned Into Apostleship by Apostle Jackie Green*
- *Humantraffickinghotlineorg*
- *Cover photo by David Munoz. Connect with him via Facebook or at Davidmunozart.com*

Kingdom Shifters Books & Apparel
Available at Kingdomshifters.com

Products available at kingdomshiftingbooks.com and amazon.com	
Books (Paperback, Kindle, and e-books available)	
Healing the Wounded Leader	There is an App for That
Apostolic Governing	Sustaining The Vision Workbook
Apostolic Mantle	Annihilating Church Hurt
Healing the Wounded Leader	Discerning the Voice of God
Release the Vision	Feasting in His Presence
Birthing Books That Shift Generations	Prayers that Shift Atmospheres
Atmosphere Changes (Weaponry)	Dismantling Homosexuality
Strategies for Eradicating Racism	Let There Be Sight
Kingdom Shifters Decree That Thang	Kingdom Watchman Builder on the Wall
Kingdom Heirs Decree That Thang	Kingdom Keys to Governing Relationships
Fivefold Operations – Manuals I, II, and III	Unmasking the Power of the Scouts – Volumes I and II
Processing Grief & Loss	Cultivating Destiny From The Womb
Kingdom Wellness Counseling & Mentoring Manual I	Deliverance From The Stronghold of Suicide
Dismantling Demonic Kingdoms Encyclopedia	Gatekeeping Regions For God's Glory
Books for Liturgical / Interpretive Dance Ministries	
Dance & Fivefold Ministry	Dance from Heaven to Earth
Spirits that Attack Dance Ministers	Dancers! Dancers! Dancers! Decree That Thang
CD's	
Decree That Thang	Kingdom Heirs Decree That Thang
Teaching and Worship	

www.ingramcontent.com/pod-product-compliance
Lightning Source LLC
Chambersburg PA
CBHW071307110426
42743CB00042B/1207